W9-AMQ-250

RIVER PLACE

RIVER
PLACE

One Man's Search For Serenity

Doug Baker

Sketches By
Jon Masterson

Timber Press   Forest Grove, Oregon

RIVER PLACE

One Man's Search For Serenity

Doug Baker
ISBN 0-917304-57-8
© Copyright 1980 by Timber Press
Printed In The United States Of America

Library of Congress Cataloging in Publication Data

Baker, Doug, 1922-
  River place

  1. Country life — Oregon. 2. Baker, Doug, 1922- 3. Oregon —
Biography. 4. Natural history — Oregon. I. Title.
F881.2.B34   979.5'009'94   [B]   79-27119
ISBN 0-917304-57-8

Timber Press
P.O. Box 92
Forest Grove, Oregon 97116

For A Certain Party
And for The Snowbird,
Two who shared the search.

Some of the pieces in this book, in somewhat different form, first appeared in the "Baker's Dozen" column of the Oregon Journal during the '70s.

Contents

Foreword

EVERY MAN OR WOMAN who ever wrote a book owes a debt to another author or perhaps a bevy of authors who came before him.

Sometimes that debt is transparently obvious; at others, it is a subconscious thing not at all apparent to the reader, but there in the back of the mind to haunt the author of the book under perusal.

I have no hesitancy in acknowledging my indebtedness for the idea behind this book. At some point in the '30s when I was a schoolboy first enraptured by the delights of my hometown library, I chanced upon a book titled "Adventures In Contentment" by a former newspaperman who wrote under the nom de plume of David Grayson. There was no sex or violence in Grayson's collection of quiet essays. There was precious little humor. Grayson's "adventures" were not to do with climbing mountains nor with pearl diving in the Arafura Sea. They were the tranquil adventures of the mind and spirit he encountered in chats with his neighbors, trysts with nature and in the business of everyday living. I have not seen a copy of "Adventures In Contentment" for nearly 40 years. Indeed, I have in recent years looked for a copy but have found none readily available. Occasionally I meet someone who recalls the book for it was a best seller in its day. Those who remember the book inevitably remember it with the same fondness we reserve for other gracious artifacts of a more innocent era.

When I first began writing pieces about the hideaway I call "River Place" for a newspaper in 1973 I realized I was to some extent or other aping the manner of Grayson's collection of reflective pieces. Naturally, I cannot hope to equal his style nor can I hope for his success.

My own book will disappoint those who are looking for the thrills of drama or the titillation of the salacious. It is a book without what the publishing world calls the "obligatory" dirty words or the clinical details of intimacy. It is meant for quiet browsing by those who have learned the satisfactions to be found in thinking upon the things in life that matter most after the baser passions have cooled.

Escapism is a subject that seems most popular during times of greatest historical stress. However, it seems likely that from earliest times man has been concerned with "getting away from it all." Some of us would escape the drudgery of onerous jobs. Others run from a less than tranquil domestic life. Still others seek nothing more than a break in the rut of routine. And a good few of us are looking for something a shade more meaningful — a place where we can experiment with a better philosophy of living, a mini-Utopia or Erewhon where we can be soothed by Nature's benison and find a measure of the serenity we know attaches to the "good life."

The "good life," of course, is difficult of definition. Each of us has his own ideas about it. Years of living convince most of us that it bears little relationship to hedonism. And yet, as I point out in this book, I'm certain there is room in it for the cashmere sweater as well as the hair shirt. Man cannot live by bread nor by penance alone.

There is, for each of us, another way of life. A Certain Party and I found ours a little more than an hour away from the city where we have a second home. It is a place of cedar and hemlock forests washed by glacial waters where the trees provide great gouts of pure oxygen and the sky burns with the blue rinse of summer. It is a place where a man can still find huge helpings of quiet and at least a soupçon of contentment.

A Certain Party and I have travelled with seven league boots for more than 30 years. We've lived in sun-drenched Australia and vacationed in picturesque Mexico. We've travelled through Europe and Asia and languished with the beachcombers on half a dozen Pacific islands. But here in the rain-washed corner of our own land we've come closest to finding our notion of "the good life." We call our niche in the scheme of things "River Place."

Evaluating A Dream

THE PRICE OF DREAMS, like the price of beef-steak, has been badly inflated in recent years.

We began our search for a piece of ground on a wild river in the late '60s. We knew exactly what we wanted. I had long been enamored of fishing. A Certain Party had already netted her first steelhead. Our years of living in Australia had given us a fill of beaches. We wanted a place "away from it all," but with access to a fishable river. We hoped to find a site not too far from the city.

Over the years of our quest we ruled out a number of streams. The Washougal offered little seclusion and the Nehalem too few fish. The Klickitat and the Deschutes were just too far from town. The east fork of the Lewis seemed too pastoral, not woodsy enough for our tastes. That still left us a number of options: the Toutle, Cowlitz, Kalama, north fork of the Lewis, Wilson, Trask, Clackamas and Sandy.

Luck played a big part in our eventual decision. In '68 we came close to buying a two-bedroom cabin on an 80-foot lot on the Kalama. The price was right, but we hesitated. It was too small a piece of land to fit the dimensions of our dream. Not long afterwards we came perilously close to buying an acre on the Trask, an acre treeless save for a clump of alder at the river's edge. There was a decaying trailer house on the site and that's what decided us against it. Neither of us has ever held trailer houses in high regard.

It was the late Joe Marcotte, an engaging French-Canadian, who finally found our river place for us. He was an elderly but indefatigable angler who spent a lot of time on the Northwest's rivers and we had asked him to keep an eye out for available river land.

One night there was a momentous telephone call from Joe. "Old Gus wants to sell his last piece of property," he said. "He hasn't advertised it yet, but it's up for sale."

We drove there the next day, spoke to the caretaker and walked about the land. Within minutes, we knew it was everything we had sought. Here was the site on which to forge a dream. The land itself was something more than five acres and something less than six. Gus, a onetime gyppo logger, had cleared two acres — enough for an orchard and a garden. (The soil was black and rich.) There were heavy woods along the river with a fine stand of old cedar. The bunkhouse which had once housed Gus's loggers still stood under two spreading trees. The whole was set in an almost windless canyon and, save for a single house on a nearby hill across the river road, offered a splendid isolation.

True, there were a few problems. There was no well and to drill one would mean an investment of at least $2,000, perhaps a lot more. Seemingly even more insurmountable was the asking price. Gus wanted a hefty sum, more than we had ever paid for anything in our lives, including the homes we had purchased. What's more, he wanted a big slice of it in hard cash as a down payment.

For a week or so I lay awake nights trying to think of a way to buy that land. There were few things I had ever wanted quite as much but I was like a youngster who has only $10 towards the $40 purchase price of a new bicycle and doesn't know where to get the balance. I thought of taking a second mortgage on my home and of selling a piece of property A Certain Party and I were holding as a retirement investment. I talked to friends about it, but received little encouragement. The obligations involved were clearly beyond our assets.

And then I seized the nettle and went to see my bank manager. I told him how much we wanted the river place and how little money we had in hand. He told me the bank had no interest in such mortgages and my heart sank. But it rose again when he said, "Why don't I just lend you the money for the down payment on your signature?" In an instant, the thing was done and we have never regretted it.

Of course, the payments, what with taxes, insurance and interest, proved to be enormous. But by cutting here and there and taking some extra jobs, we were able to meet them each month and, after five years, we were as well out of the financial woods as we were entrenched in our forest hideaway.

There are those who tell me (one of them is the tax assessor) that our land today is worth five or six times what we paid for it in 1971. Such talk means little as we've never thought seriously of selling. We bought River Place to hold and enjoy and to pass on to our children when we are gone, not to turn a profit. And price tags on dreams are a bad idea anyway.

Time Out From Drifting

Addison's Happy Man

"NOTHING TO DO" is a plaint of the young. As we grow older there is always too much to do — the business of getting and spending, the eternal repair jobs around the house, the social amenities required by our human relationships, the questions of duty to community and fellow man, the books to be read, the letters unwritten and the clock always running faster than can any of us.

It's that way at River Place, but here there is a difference. Whatever we do takes on an altered coloration. No job is truly distasteful nor onerous. Every task is a joy. If one wearies of a pursuit, he drops it for a time and turns to another. The challenges are stimulating without being overwhelming. And what is not done today is easily put off for another day in a nebulous future.

One of my friends is fond of quoting Joseph Addison's wisdom that "the grand essentials to happiness in this life are something to do, something to love and something to hope for." In the woods we have all three in abundance. There is so much to do, so much to love and always the hope that somehow the happiness will endure.

Beyond all that, there are the lessons which only Nature can teach. I know a fellow who went to one of those experiments in communal living in California where people sit around naked contemplating their own and then each other's navels. They call it "group therapy" or "sensitivity training" and this fellow who went down there said it helped him to "get his head on straight." When you spend a lot of time in the woods and on the river your head fits quite straight enough without all that folderol.

The small pleasures are surely the greatest pleasures. We take pleasure in watching the rabbits play their games of tag in the wet grass before dusk, observing the grouse which run ahead of us on the dirt road along Snowbird's ridge and studying the hummingbirds at the feeders outside the cabin, Nature's sneer at the aerodynamics engineers who say it is impossible for them to fly, a reminder that the slide rule is not invincible.

We watch snakes collecting bugs in the orchard grass and the blackbirds which scavenge for scraps left by the chickens. We move tiny seedlings from the deep woods and replant them where they can catch the sun. We visit the henhouse four or five times a day just to see how the broody hen is doing with her eggs. The calendar says she has been set only 20 days, but we look for the chicks anyway. Yet, there is no hurrying Nature. Next morning, promptly on the 21st day, we find the nest full of empty shells and little balls of fluff already scratching for their first breakfasts.

A Certain Party has caught some great steelhead in the falls below the cabin, but I have yet to take one there. Most of my fishing has been done from the drift boat and, with all the building we're doing, there's been too little of that.

But our weekend guests have departed and there are still several hours of daylight now that the days are longer. The rain is little more than a gentle veil, so I pull on my hip waders and rig a spinning rod with a copper spinner.

For an hour or more I work the white water below the falls with no results save the loss of three spinners. I walk back to the boatshed to look for more and I find an old nickel-plated spoon with a single siwash hook.

Back at the river I move downstream to where the current plays over a single giant rock in relatively quiet water. On my third cast above the rock I feel two quick tugs on the spoon and I set the hook hard. A swatch of silver jets into the air and falls back. The fish jumps again, this time like a marlin. I yell to A Certain Party to bring the net from the boathouse and she races up the bank in her heavy rubber boots as the fish breaks water for the third time.

For 10 minutes I play the fish carefully, letting him make his runs against an easy drag, reeling him against the current only when he slacks off. A Certain Party is nowhere to be seen and I fear that my light leader will surely break if I do not bring him to the bank soon.

Finally, I can wait no longer for the net and I nurse the big silver fish to the bank. He struggles, but comes ashore, a beautiful shining thing of at least eight and perhaps 10 pounds. I reach for a rock to give him the coup de grace and he makes a final flip, breaking the leader. For an instant, he lies there, free, at the water's edge and I make a last grab for him, but he is far too quick and I am far too slow. In a flash, he is gone.

I have lost a lot of steelhead, but never one that meant quite so much to me. Maybe it was because he fought so well, I walk up the path to the cabin and I meet A Certain Party coming down. She had found the boatshed locked and I had the keys. She, too, had her moment of frustration.

For a time, I am desolate. But then I think of that

beautiful fish working the lure from his jaws on the river bottom and living either to fight another day or to make his odyssey once again to the sea. For me, there will be other fish and other disappointments. I am suddenly glad that a fish that fought so well escaped me. And I am acutely aware that the happiness found in angling lies not so much with the catch as with the quest. Like Addison's happy man, I am left with something for which to hope.

The Well Witcher

WE ARE LOSING our spring drinking water which comes cold and clear from an outcropping on the property adjoining ours down river. It has apparently served this place well for many years, but there has been a change of ownership and we must find a new source of water.

Early in the morning the man comes about the new well. He is an expansive, outgoing man with a zest for selling not only wells but pumps, tanks, water softeners, pipes and a dozen related gadgets. He has a look around our acreage and then he sits down in our cabin over coffee to figure an estimate.

"It costs $6 a foot to dig a well," he says. "That's for the first 100 feet. After that it gets more expensive, maybe $7 a foot. You'll need a pump and a tank. If we get water within 100 feet it will run to $1,357."

"What if you strike water at 50 feet?" I ask.

"Then you'll save $300 and I'll be able to sell you something else. If you get a lot of iron you're going to need a filter and a water softener."

We make the deal. The salesman turns to go, but pauses on the threshold. "What about a witcher?" he asks.

A Certain Party and I are more than skeptical. After all, there's no scientific basis for water witching. This is 1971 and people don't believe in voodoo anymore. Or do they?

"I don't believe in it myself," says the salesman. "But I wouldn't drill a well without one. I put one down without a witcher one time and the customer spent $2,700 on a bad hole. Finally got a witcher and the fellow got good water right away."

There's a contradiction in this most likely based on the fact the salesman gets a hunk of the witcher's fee, but I'm too polite to mention it. "How much?" I ask.

"Most of 'em charge $25," says the salesman. "Our fellow charges $35, but if you don't get water he gives you your money back."

Just as I'd figured, there's an extra $10 in it for the salesman. But I don't quibble.

* * *

SUNDAY MORNING right after we watched two crows dive bombing a hawk that had invaded their territorial demesne, the salesman comes up our driveway with his witcher.

The witcher is an elderly man with a sunburnt face and bib overalls. He carries a forked willow branch and has another in his hip pocket. He's not one for social amenities. Without a word, he begins walking up and down in front of the cabin, holding his willow magic before him.

"What's his name?" I ask the salesman. After all, if you're going to spend $35 doing business with a professional man, you're entitled to know his identity.

"Herb Moore," says the salesman. Of course. It would have to be Herb or Silas or Hank or one of the other names redolent of backwoods Vermont or rural Indiana. One wouldn't expect a water witcher to have a city slicker sort of name.

Herb makes two or three quick passes across the pasturage we've begun calling the orchard. He pauses now and then to rub a mark into the earth with the edge of a boot where he says there's a vein of subterranean water. After three or four minutes he gets a "real strong pull" behind the logging shed and says that's the best place to drill for water.

"How does it work?" I ask him. Herb says he doesn't know. He does volunteer that he used to witch wells for free until he retired from his job as a power lineman seven years ago. He lets A Certain Party hold one end of his willow branch and when he holds hands with her the branch unfailingly swings over towards the earth. He lets me try it. Nothing. A real skeptic doesn't have the power of the faith, I guess.

"Won't work for me, either," says the expansive salesman. "Only about one in 10 can do it."

Five or six minutes after his arrival, Herb pockets his fee which is only $25 after all. I don't question the discrepancy and Herb says nothing about a money-back guarantee, either. You don't question such matters when you're dealing with a professional man.

Next week the crew will start drilling for water. We still won't be sure if witching works or not, but we'll know if it doesn't work and that, I guess, is something.

Two Happy River Rats

Time Of The Harvest Moon

LABOR DAY BRINGS a wading army of anglers to the lower reaches of the river, but our little cabin is miles upstream and we fish in splendid isolation.

The big run of long-waited silvers moved up the rain-muddied stream in earnest on Sunday and those with fortitude enough to risk a drenching under leaden skies easily filled their punch cards.

It is a good run this year. The silverside salmon are fat and bright and with them come the sea-run cutthroat or harvest trout as well as the jack salmon. And there is always the chance of an occasional steelhead.

Our neighbor, Charlie, comes with the news. "The run is on," he says. "I've got eight fish in the box already. I must have had 15 on this morning but I only landed two."

A Certain Party and Snowbird are agog with Charlie's report. They busy themselves with leader and lead and eggs. They pull on their long hip boots and find the walking sticks they use for balance when clambering over the mossy rocks below the falls.

They are the two most indefatigable fisherwomen I have ever known. Most women don't care for fishing at all. A minority don't mind angling for trout or bass

when the sun is warm. But my women fish in all weathers
and hang with it until the water runs down their backs.

* * *

THERE IS AN ODD division of labor in our family
this summer. The women fish for hours each weekend,
but Snowbird's husband and I are lucky to get in a few
minutes of such sport at the end of the day.

It is the business of building or, more properly, rebuilding the cabin. Jon has drawn a princely design, but the
work never seems to end. Not only must we frame and
panel and shake and wire and plumb, but there are all
the incidental jobs.

The well drillers found a solid vein of water — 12
to 15 gallons per minute — at 152 feet. Now there
is a waterline to lay and the long trench for it yet to
be dug. The wellhouse is yet to be built. Charlie dug
us an enormous pit for our 900-gallon septic tank, but
the drainfield remains unexcavated.

There are the endless trips to town for supplies. Work
in the fresh air develops enormous appetites and we are
always short of bread or milk or coffee, or another piece
of No. 10 wire.

Ours is a cooperative project with communal over-
tones. Charlie does the heavy framing and plumbing and
shifts the earth when he's not hauling sand or gravel
in his old truck. My brother does the wiring and helps
Charlie with the heavier lifting.

Jon is great with the windows and doors and the trim.
He finds old curved windows in wrecking yards and
grouts them into place under the steeply-pitched roof.
The women help with the sanding and painting and
the cabin gradually nears some semblance of completion.
But it is doubtful that we can finish by fall and serious
fishing will have to wait for another season.

* * *

MEANWHILE, there are moments when we can get

away from the toil and enjoy the charm peculiar to life in the woods.

The chipmunks are gone from the tool shed now. The hazelnuts have been ripe in the forest for several weeks and I suppose they no longer have need of our puny handouts.

But other creatures have come to take their place. A tiny mouse with a giant head lives in one of the tool drawers. When I open the drawer I am careful not to disturb him and he doesn't seem to mind the intrusion. Snowbird says he is a "kangaroo mouse" and others insist he is a shrew.

The bats are another matter. They resent our presence in the tool shed and fly about over our heads in tight circles. Just before dark they take to the sky to harvest the insects.

All the deer seem to have been spooked. One was killed by a logging truck last week and since then we catch only a glimpse now and then of a doe coming to the river for water in the evening. The sapsuckers, too, have gone from the birch tree. Even the swallows have moved on.

But there are always new dwellers moving in. A brace of pelicans have shown up along the river, along with a covey of mergansers. The hunters have scared away the bandtail pigeons, but an occasional grouse still lingers in the deep woods.

The harvest moon over the weekend was a silvery orb playing hide-and-seek behind the tall hemlocks. It bathed the woods in ghostly light and we kept breaking up our game of hearts just to have one more look at it. Jon's high curved windows are great for moon watching.

There are, of course, a few hazards and discomforts. Snowbird's dog, Earl, got into some fresh salmon and nearly died before a vet pulled him through a bout of fish poisoning. Our arms are punctured with no-see-um bites and several of our volunteer helpers have suffered bruised fingers and saw cuts.

But generally, it is a healthful, happy life, far from the tensions and carbon monoxide of the city. We think of it as a semi-secret place where the few neighbors are friendly and the chickens find bonanzas in the rotting stumps and the river sings its eternal song, a melody at once urgent and yet timeless. It is a haven snug against telephones and trauma and a spot where a man can go to bed dog-tired after a day of mixing concrete, knowing that he has found something as close to serenity as life can offer in a troubled age.

No Solid Waste Problems

IF AUTUMN COMES, winter is surely hard on its heels and there is much work to do on the cabin if we are to keep warm and dry through the gray months of drizzle.

It isn't easy to concentrate on the work because the woods are aflame with color and the call of the river is strong. The big maples drop their scraggy leaves until the rapids run yellow with their decaying beauty. And high on the hills the smaller vine maples crimson the morning mists.

But we must have an eavestrough if we are to keep the rain from gathering under the little cabin. My friendly neighbor, Charlie, helps me cut the gutter and caulk it.

The man finally came to drop the pump deep into the new well, but the well house needs insulation against the danger of freezing weather. The cabin, too, takes a lot of insulating and we use oakum to fill the chinks around the doors and windows. There are literally a hundred things to do, but somehow they get done if one keeps at it.

* * *

EACH WEEK the woods offer a new surprise. This

time it was seeing my first beaver.

I have seen their traces often enough. Drifting down the river the saplings on which they have been gnawing are a common sight on the mud banks, cleanly peeled and slick with sharpened ends.

But the beaver is a furtive creature, keeping his distance from man. It is not unusual to surprise an otter, particularly when our Rogue drift boat is gliding quietly around a bend in the river. You quite often see them playing on the rocks or diving into the shallows.

This particular morning I took four hours off from building to drift the river with an uncle who had never caught a steelhead. No sooner had we launched the boat than we saw this large shape moving in a still pool. At first glance I took it for a spawning salmon. But no, it was clearly a beaver with its wide flat tail propelling it upstream.

* * *

MY UNCLE ROBERT caught his first steelhead. So did my cousin, a high school boy who was with us.

It is a bit late in the season for summer fish, but these struck hard and clean and fought well before I took them in the big land net. They were both females with just a trace of color.

One of the great things about drifting in a boat for steelhead is that even when you catch no fish you have had the pleasure and excitement of running the river. There are always birds and animals to be seen and the rapids can be more exciting at times than any carnival ride.

But when you put two fish into the boat and hook into several more which you lose in the chase, you have had an extraordinary day. My cup runneth over.

* * *

OUR COUNTY'S League of Women Voters held a luncheon the other day in the small town where we go for supplies. "Come to our luncheon and discuss solid waste problems," said the signs advertising the event.

The signs also billed two speakers, one a county commissioner and the other a "solid waste coordinator," whatever in the name of all that's unpolluted that might be.

I have some trouble imagining a group of women, even the most civic-minded, sitting around over plates of fried chicken discussing solid waste. And I don't mean to be chauvinistic. Not only women, but men should find something more attractive to discuss over lunch, even if it's a business deal, an insurance policy or yesterday's golf game or the baby's colic. Solid waste? Surely, such a momentous issue belongs to an after-dinner meeting or a morning session with coffee.

It seems as though once you've had three or four days of quiet in the woods, even the small towns seem too big. The trouble is that small towns, like big towns, tend to have women sitting around at luncheon discussing solid waste problems. The problem is real enough and I don't mean to belittle it or the "solid waste coordinator" dying to discuss it.

But we have no waste problems at River Place. We feed most of the garbage to the chickens and bury deep in the earth those things that will not burn. Sure, we are aware of the growing need for better ways to handle mankind's burgeoning mountain of refuse. On the other hand, we don't wish to talk about it at luncheon.

One of my deer hunting neighbors up river gave me a package of venison backstrap and that is my luncheon. I fix it Viennese style with sour cream and red currant jelly and I talk to Charlie about how much pitch to give the eaves, how well the pullets are laying and the big beaver we saw in the quiet pool above the falls. When I get back to city there'll be time enough to join the ladies as they talk of garbage dumps and rusting junkers.

Ducks Unimpressed With
The Little Red Truck

No Goblins
For Halloween

THE ELK HUNTERS move up the road in a continual parade of pick-ups, their well-oiled rifles glistening on gun racks. They remind me a bit more of Texans than of Northwesterners.

But so far they all seem to have come back down the road without any kills. A Certain Party is glad because although she has no strong bias against hunting for meat, she hates seeing the beautiful elk draped across the fenders of a truck for all the world to see. It's even worse when the mighty hunters sever the head and mount it atop the truck like something to scare the children on Halloween.

The deer which moved through our yard so tamely last summer are long gone. We imagine them hiding in the deep brush where few hunters care to go. The hunters park on the back country roads along the ridges and play their car radios and drink bourbon from bottles kept in brown paper bags. They know the deer are sticking to the brush, but they have small appetite for thistle, blackberry and wet browse. They sit all day in their warm cabs, hoping a deer will wander their way from cover so they can get their meat the easy way.

This time of year I am usually in the wheat stubble

of Eastern Washington, but this year my shotgun stays
in the closet. It seems that after 35 years of hunting
pheasant, quail and partridge, I have lost my appetite
for the sport. My bird dog is 13 or 14 now and too
old for the field. And while I insist I'm still young enough
for chasing upland game, it would appear that I have
become too mellow.

* * *

WHATEVER ZEST I have for killing for the table
I spend on the steelhead. It is crisply chill these mornings
and the river runs high after a week of showers. But
the water is surprisingly clear and we can see the steelhead lurking in the deep pools as we tow our drift boat
upstream.

Once in the boat we find a confraternity which bridges
age and occupation and mode of living. Jon is an artist
with long hair and a savage swatch of beard. He mans
the oars and moves the boat through the swift drifts
below the rapids where the fish like to rest. Orville is
a police officer of cleanshaven visage and it might be
asking too much for a marriage of philosophy in a drift
boat freighted by three men of disparate backgrounds
and outlooks.

But in our quest of the fish we are a team. Like all
good fishermen, our appreciation of the sport goes far
beyond the taking of the fish which come still glistening
in silver from the water even on the last day of October
with just a streak of rouge along their sides to show they
are summer run.

We thrill to startled blue herons and curious water
ouzels and the mergansers which race before the boat.
In the mist-shrouded hills, draped with wet hemlock and
fir, Jon sees "Chinese landscape painting." Orville and
I see only the beauty of a late October morning, but
we share the wonder of surroundings yet unsullied by
the filth of man.

BELOW A SMALL CREEK which spills like the Spanish Steps of Rome into our river, Orville gets the first hook-up. It is a small steelhead and offers little resistance. But a few minutes later the same pool yields three scrappy harvest trout in succession.

Another mile or so down river, Orville hooks into the first big steelhead. His rod bends smartly as the lure hits home and then come the frantic runs and leaps as the fish makes its desperate bid for freedom. When you have fished steelhead for some years you know the ritual can have only one of two endings and yet it is never quite the same. Each fish is different just as no two stretches of river are equal. There are always those fish that outwit or outfight the fisherman. And there are those which come to the net quickly to be dispatched with weighted club.

On this late day in autumn the great salmon are mostly just dead hulks on which the crayfish feed. But here and there a few of the monsters continue to thresh out the gravelly nests for their eggs, lashing with their tails to perform rites that seem at once beautifully primeval and ineffably sad.

Back at the cabin, Orville and I clean our much-admired catch, carefully saving the roe for fish bait. We lock the dogs inside while we clean the fish for the fresh blood is lethal to canines because of some quirk of Nature.

After the fish are cleaned and ready for the smoker we walk down to the river and make our way along an old log bridge greasy with wet maple leaves to watch Jon and his friend, Bruce, slalom their kayaks through the rapids while Snowbird takes picures. It is scarcely mid-afternoon, but the clocks have been set back and the sky is close and dark and the days in the woods are now far too short. No time today for any more work on the cabin, but it is snug enough and the finishing will keep.

Darkness falls swiftly and a kind neighbor sends us a pumpkin pie and Snowbird fries slices of big red potatoes and warms a can of roast beef. We all eat too well and share a bottle of red wine and then play cribbage, two at a time while the others kibitz the game and yawn and step outside now and then to watch for a trace of moon in the wet sky. There are no goblins in the woods, real or fancied, even on Halloween. The dogs are asleep after a day of romping and the only sound is the eternal rush of the river which never sleeps.

The Laudanum Of Winter

WINTER BRINGS a kind of torpor to the woods. The wind and rain have undressed the trees and the hunters have finished with their harvest, leaving our little patch of solitude as quiet and stark as we have seen it.

Not only are the deer and chipmunks long gone, but we look vainly for glimpse of squirrels or otter. The rain-washed sky is empty of bats and birds and it's almost as though there is a plague on the land.

But along the river we still see the friendly ouzel. He is a cheery sight on the dark, drizzle-shrouded days and it is small wonder he's known as the "fisherman's friend." The ouzel reminds us that there is always beauty here, even in the months of cold and wet.

And beautiful it is. The laudanum of winter may stay the new leaf and bud, but it cannot suppress the grandeur of hills, velvety green and soft with patches of brilliant snow above us, looking down as the churning river sings a robust January song.

* * *

IT IS THE NATURE of the river to be ever changing. In late August and September we could almost wade across at the falls and the angler could search out every pocket with fly or spinner.

But January's river is a torrent, tumescent with melt-ing snow and freighted with rain. The falls are all but buried in a frenzy of water and the ruins of the logging bridge, once a good place from which to cast a bait, are off limits because the timbers have shifted and are no longer secure.

Prized fishing spots are inundated and wadable eddies are no longer wadable, even in thigh high boots. A Cer-tain Party still tries her hand at fishing with fresh roe, but only the high ground above the little rocky beach offers her a place on which to stand. Because the water is so charged with mud, chances of a strike are lean.

But we have better luck with the boat. We work the muddied drifts over and over and we find fish with sheer perseverance when lazier fishermen fail. Because the cur-rent runs so strong it means a lot of rowing and tired shoulders at the end of the day. But the winter fish are bright and fat and worth the extra effort. The males make fine eating and the females yield long orange skeins of eggs for the bait freezer before they go into the smoker.

* * *

TWO FOOTBALL TEAMS met Sunday in some-thing grandiosely styled the "Super Bowl" and for a time, spackling plasterboard and nailing up trim in the cabin, I had the idea that I might be the only adult male in the entire land not huddled before a TV set.

But then my neighbor, Charlie, came down from the hill across the road to talk and I learned that he, too, had no idea how the Miami Dolphins might be faring. People who live in the woods have less need for such opiates. There is always kindling to be split and slab firewood to be stacked. There is a need to keep an eye on the weather and to wonder about a possible freeze. And there is a kind of loneliness which makes a man reach out for his neighbors. You don't find these things in front of a lighted box in a darkened room. Besides all that, the television reception here in the canyon is a sorry thing.

Charlie's wife, Juanita, is one of those women who are happiest when feeding others. She sends Charlie down to our place with great slabs of pie and casseroles of chicken. If we stop by Charlie's house we leave with pans of cinnamon rolls and chunks of smoked salmon. Juanita likes phonograph records by such artists as Wayne Newton and the Moms and Dads. Charlie isn't much for music, but he likes to sit and talk and nurse a lipful of snoose by a big roaring fire and tell me of the mistakes I have made in building the cabin.

It is remote country where Charlie's is the only telephone for more than a mile around and people come to his door late at night when their cars are stranded in the snows of the mountains above him or someone without a telephone needs a doctor. In a region where most nocturnal visitors are greeted by snarling dogs and landholders toting shotguns, it is good to have a few friendly Charlies.

The day of the football game was gray and wet and not a bad day at all for doing odd jobs inside with Charlie around to point out better ways of doing them. A Certain Party put on her sou'wester and oilskins and inched her way along the boiling river in hopes of finding a fish and couldn't have cared less that millions of Americans were snug and warm in their living rooms watching a football game. I suppose when I get back to the city I'll find a newspaper and then I'll know who won.

"Charlie's not short. He's just built
a little closer to the ground than most men."

Charlie's $763 Pole

MY SNOOSE-CHEWING FRIEND, Charlie McGinnis, is a truthful sort of fellow in the important things of life, but like most people who've lived long years in the woods he's been accused from time to time of embellishing an unimportant yarn.

It's a quiet life here in the river country and nobody can blame a fellow over much for adding a tiny bit of drama to his stories.

Hence, when a logging truck forced Charlie off the river road a few weeks ago and Charlie's car snapped off a utility pole, I wasn't quite sure that I should believe Charlie's version of his bill from the public utility district.

After all, Charlie had the worst end of an accident that he said wasn't his fault. His car had been totaled, his left hand was bruised and, a few days after the mishap, he went to a hospital for eight blood transfusions because the blow to his abdomen had activated a quiescent ulcer, causing him to bleed internally. The driver of the log truck had kept on going and the log truck drivers behind him said they didn't know the identity of the driver who had forced Charlie into the ditch and pole. Logging truck drivers, like a lot of other occupational groups, tend to stick together.

The public utility district, Charlie told me, was going to charge him a bundle for breaking their pole. I was skeptical until Charlie showed me the invoice.

It seems as though it took a foreman and five helpers the best part of six hours to undo the damage. A foreman on overtime, I learned from the invoice, gets $20 an hour. That was $120.

One of the linemen worked 13 hours of overtime, said the PUD, and his tab was $231.14. A straight time lineman claimed $35.56 for four hours. A "head groundman" charged $92.40 for his six hours of overtime and two lesser "groundmen" collected $78.96 and $75.12.

Truck expenses for a pick-up, a front wheel drive, a ManLift and a ladder truck came to $75.60. The pole itself, a 45-footer, cost $74.84. There was a 20-inch bolt at $1.64 and some insulators at $3.45 plus some other hardware.

All in all, the cost of the new pole came to $792.20.

But the PUD is nothing if not fair. They made an allowance of $29 for the "depreciation" of the pole and accoutrements destroyed in the accident. Thus, Charlie owes the PUD only $763.20, a miniscule figure which should please his insurance company.

But Charlie does have a gripe. He could have used the broken pole for firewood on these long winter nights. The PUD wouldn't let him have it.

It's enough to make a mountain man like Charlie swallow his snoose.

High Water
And Freezing Pipes

OLDTIMERS DISAGREE about the cold, but there seems to be consensus about the flooding. "The river hasn't been that high since '33," they say, and I am prone to believe them.

Now that the flooding is done and the river is back in its winter channel it is easy enough to assess the damage. Our cabin remains high and dry, but there are others on the river who weren't so lucky. We hear of damage to pilings and foundations and of the two horses swept away in the current that was as strong as a blind man's rage. They found the horses four days after the river rose — one just scared and hungry, but the other dead.

The swollen river tore at the old log bridge below us and finally ripped two of the giant logs from their rotting moorings. Goodness knows how many years they have lain there, a relic of gyppo logging days that seemed immovable and a marvelous place from which to watch the fishing at the falls.

Spring's new growth will hide most of the scars left by the flood and time will erase the rest. This past week it's cold, not flooding, that dominates conversation on the river.

Some of the oldtimers say the temperature dropped to nine degrees. Others say it couldn't have been any colder than 11 degrees. I record both figures in my cabin journal, but am more concerned with the problems caused by the freeze than with its nadir.

When I built the new addition to the cabin last summer I put it on piers. Now, I know that was unwise and when winter is gone I shall have to put a foundation under it.

Charlie has told me often that water pipes never freeze in this hollow. He has been here for more than a decade and it's a surprise to him to find his water system is frozen as solidly as is mine.

I had "banked" the cabin with boards and earth when the cold weather came and it wasn't easy to get under it this past week. I found the earth frozen solid for six inches or more and had to use a pick axe to break it. Once underneath the dwelling, I found long icicles hanging from the drainpipes. None of the pipes seem broken, which is a blessing. But they are obviously jammed with ice. Charlie and I tried old remedies such as boiling water, but nothing seemed to shift the frozen mass. I boarded up the foundation again and rebanked it with the frozen dirt. When the warm rains come, it will clear.

"First time I've ever known it to freeze," reflected Charlie, taking a big dip out of his can of Copenhagen. Yeah, I chided him, it's a real banana belt up here. He laughed and we went up to his place for coffee and cheese sandwiches. Before long it was time to go back to the city and I drove slowly along the river road where huge sheets of ice hung in weird shapes from the banks and ice formed on the road in patches. I stopped by one of the springs and had a drink so cold it hurt my teeth. I saw a few boats drifting the river, the fishermen holding their rods awkwardly in their mittens, the ice forming in the guides on their rods and stiffening their landing nets. I've been on the river on days not much different and I know how it is. Every guy in the boat wants to do the rowing because it is the only way of keeping warm.

Roy and Charlie, the Hollow's Most Durable Characters.

Learning
About The Woods

THERE IS A SMALL white house on the edge of our property at River Place which apparently dates to the late '20s or early '30s when this was still a logging headquarters.

When we bought our acreage the old house was tenanted by an aging man named Roy Gotham, a difficult codger with a National Rifle Association sticker on the rear window of his Nash, a derringer in his pocket and a headful of strange notions about the country going to the dogs because of the "international Jewish bankers."

We always had mixed feelings about Roy. He looked after our flock of chickens when we were in the city with great care and the skill of a countryman. Each weekend he would produce a pail full of the eggs he had gathered and say, "Am I not a good chickenkeeper?" He made an excellent watchman, perhaps too good a watchman because we heard disturbing tales from Charlie about Roy blasting away with a shotgun whenever someone drove into our place for unexplained reasons late at night. And there was a particularly vexing story that Roy had, on at least one occasion, "pulled his derringer" in an argument with some trespassers.

Anyway, Roy was a difficult case and we weren't overly sorry when, after a lot of complaints about the nomin-
al $25 a month rent we were charging him, he decided
to pull up stakes and head for Michigan where, he said,
he had a sister he hadn't seen in years.

But the new tenants we got for the white house proved
even less satisfactory. They were a couple best described
as "hippies" and strictly urban types with no knowledge
whatever of country life. They cared little for feeding
the chickens and even less about trespassers. The girl
was ill much of the time and her husband, unable to
cope with a woodstove and an ailing wife, gave up on
River Place and packed up the girl and their few belong-
ings and moved on.

So it is that Roy, who's been fretting in a motel in
town, is back again. He is 78 now and moves slowly,
but despite all his crotchets it is good to have him around
once more.

We walked along the river Sunday and Roy read a
wealth of information from the tracks in the snow. "You
see those coyote tracks," he said. "That's why we're not
seeing any rabbits around." I asked him how he could
tell coyote tracks from dog tracks and he gave me the
withering look he reserves for my dumber questions.

The deer tracks were plain enough. Even a dude such
as I can recognize them. The deer have been forced down
from the high places by the heavy snows and like to
browse in the blackberry vines in the woods behind my
horseshoe court.

Near the water's edge there was a thin film of snow
and Roy spotted the tell-tale signs left by the river creatures. "See that tail mark?" he asked. "That's a beaver."

A minute later he found some very tiny prints.
"Mink," he said. "I saw them here last summer and they
had some young."

The river is relatively quiet again and jade in color

instead of yellow, but it seemed too cold for fishing. When the river drops quickly with the cold and stays cold, the steelhead become inert, hugging the bottom, uninterested in lures or bait.

We walked back through the woods which were quiet except for the crunch of our boots on the ice and the rustle of those tiny birds which are like wrens only browner and plumper, like tiny puffballs of explosive energy. Even Roy didn't know their name and I made a mental note to look them up in the bird book.

I had a glass of bourbon with Roy to take off the chill and told him I was glad he was back. And I am glad — if only he will eschew talking politics and not resume his carping about the rent. Because he is a difficult man, it may be good for me to humor him and remember that he is old. At least, in the woods, it is easier to live with such difficulties than it would be in the city where a man's peccadilloes tend too often to be a cause of anger rather than a source of humor.

Jubal Joins The Gang

March Brings
Warm Winds

BASEMENT CLEANING may nurture whatever it is in us that yearns for hairshirt activity, but after a day or two of it the lure of river and woods breaks through the most Spartan resolution.

It's not for the fishing, goodness knows. The rain beats on the tin roof of the old cabin with the persistence, as John Barrymore once said, of an unpaid madam. Rivulets of water course down the hill and past the chickenhouse. The nameless creek brims with surface water and the river itself, swollen near flood stage again, takes on the silty look of boarding house coffee. Fishing under such circumstances is certifiable lunacy.

Muddied waters serve in a way to remind us that the river and the woods which hug the banks will endure. The wind that blows the rain comes warm, almost as warm as the Chinook of the prairies.

Each day the cabin grows tighter and the big thermometer outside the bedroom window reflects the rising temperatures. Standards change in the woods. In the 40s we work outdoors with no real discomfort. In the 50s it seems almost balmy. And when the mercury touches 60, as it has most days the past week or two, it is veritable shirtsleeve weather.

The days and nights now are fecund with expectancy. The does are heavy with their fawns and will drop them in a month or six weeks. A few more months and they'll be coming to mooch apples from those on the river who keep no dogs.

Incipient spring has already tipped the willow with delicate greens and the young trees in our small orchard are taking root quickly and sending out new buds like tiny flags to herald the change. The climbing strawberries are pushing through their winter blankets of dried hay.

The swallows came back two or three nights ago and we could hear them tittering in the dark long before we saw them at dawn. Old Roy knew they were almost due and he was ready for them. One of our seven pullets had died during the week. Roy and Charlie examined it closely for weasel marks and concluded that it had died of natural causes. Roy picked the plumage so the swallows would have ample material for nest-building. There is a fluidity about ecology in the country of which the city dweller knows little.

Garlic, rhubarb, daffodil and iris are all showing themselves and the first really sunny day will bring March flowers. The big currant bush beside the horseshoe court is almost indecently pregnant and has become the calendar which, surely one day this week, will mark winter's unmourned funeral.

There are compensations for every negative. While the coffee-colored water means no fishing, it means more time for finishing work on the cabin.

As there was last autumn, there is a communal effort this spring. Uncle Orville puts the finishing touches to the wiring and we finally have power outlets in all the rooms. The Snowbird and Jon found some knotty Ponderosa pine at a bargain price and the old cabin had a handsome new ceiling. Charlie came from the hill to help me hang a new door which I bought secondhand for $5 and there is a fine new view window which Jon bought and installed for us as a Christmas gift.

A Certain Party is busy hanging drapes and curtains and we realize that in all the cedar and pine there is a need for color. The Snowbird and ACP take turns with paint brush and Chinese red and now the big new door and one of the windows glow with swatches of scarlet.

Sheldon is kept busy picking up the scrap lumber and keeping the burn barrel going. Charlie's wife comes to see how the work is going and she brings with her a big batch of hot cinnamon rolls from her industrious oven. We stop work for coffee and a chat and then are back at it again.

But in the evening when we are all tired there is a time for quiet games. Because our TV reception is so poor here in the hollow ringed by high hills, we have learned the simple pleasures of entertaining ourselves. We play anagrams and Scrabble and contract bridge and still get up at cockcrow to feed the chickens and check on the river and begin another day of building. Now and then we hear something of the doings in New Hampshire or Florida, but they seem of small import when there is trim to be sanded or new shelves to be sawed and nailed. The news in the woods is of smaller, less grand events than political primaries. Finding a few sprigs of watercress for the salad looms far bigger than Muskie's bid for a presidential nomination and that, I would think, is the way it should be when a man is searching for a few days of serenity.

The Charm
Of Idyllic May

WHEN WE WERE first married and scratching to make ends meet like flies at a vegetarian picnic, we lived in a simple little house with crude furniture, scant plumbing and few creature comforts.

But we were happy just to have a roof in those days of wartime shortages and I don't think we ever gave a thought to how poor we must have seemed to others until one day a friend from a wealthy family came to call.

He stood there looking at the worn linoleum on the floor and the badly stained kitchen sink and I knew he was casting about for the tactful word to describe it all. And he found it.

"It must be an idyllic existence," he said. Idyllic. A pastoral word. The man who can think of such a word in such a situation is truly gifted.

It is a word that comes to mind often along the river now that our giant dogwood is in flower and the woods are filled with the sights and sounds of springtime's wonder.

Idyllic. Suggesting an idyll. That which is picturesque or pleasing in its natural simplicity. How better to describe the charm of late April and early May in the Northwest?

* * *

PICTURESQUE is surely the adjective for the show Roy performs for us between the shop and the boatshed. He has a sackful of white feathers and he looses them, one by one, into the gentlest of zephyrs which barely stirs the air of this deep hollow. Roy is approaching 80 and while he is capable of bouts of cantankerousness, he also can be infinitely kind. He is a sort of grandfather to the chipmunks and rabbits and other wild things that come to River Place in the spring.

He is particularly fond of the swallows. He builds house after house for them, nailing them under the eaves of his little home and along the roof of the shop. Last August when the heat drove the young swallows gasping from their nests he would rush about the yard rescuing the fallen birds and tenderly put them back in their boxes.

But for the past week Roy has been helping the swallows with their nest building. Almost before each white feather leaves his hand, it is snatched up by a swooping, darting bird. One of the violet greens, more aggressive than the larger barn swallows, gets more than its share of the building material and there are a few fights. But it is a splendid show that goes on and on until all Roy's feathers are gone.

* * *

THE SWALLOWS were accustomed to nesting in the loft of our old cabin and this spring when we put new siding on the structure it was necessary to block their entrance.

Roy was concerned about the swallows that usually nested there. (They even have a nest in an old aluminum saucepan someone once tacked against a knothole in the boatshed.) Accordingly, he built a new swallow house and nailed it under the eaves by the back porch of the cabin.

Charlie came down for a visit, bringing Mrs. Charlie with him. She is a splendid cook and a kind soul, but full of the fanciful notions of country folk.

"You've got to get rid of that swallow cage," said Mrs. Charlie. "They're full of lice and they bring bedbugs."

Her concern seemed farfetched, but Mrs. Charlie is sometimes right when we think her foolish. Just to be sure I checked with Dave Marshall, regional biologist for the U.S. Wildlife Refuges and a good ornithologist.

"Sure," said Marshall, "swallows have lice. But they're feather lice, not people lice. Bedbugs? No. Frankly, I'd like having swallows around my house. They're extremely good insectivores, you know."

Yes, we know they eat a lot of insects. What with the swallows and the chickens and the dozens of small snakes that run in the long grass we're bothered very little with insect pests.

The swallow box near the back door may be a minor inconvenience Surely, however, we'll be disturbing the swallows more than they'll be disturbing us. I think the box is there to stay.

* * *

NATURE IS PLEASING in many ways now that spring is here. There is great excitement in the hollow over the appearance of yet a new pair of bald eagles nesting in a tall, broken fir.

Charlie tries to point out the eagle nest to me, high on the escarpment we now call Snowbird Ridge because our daughter has bought it and plans one day to build a hideaway there. But I cannot see it, even with the binoculars.

Everyone but me has seen the eagles. A Certain Party has seen them and Mrs. Charlie sees them every day. Maybe I am too busy with the building chores. I did not hear the ruffled grouse drumming down by the creek this morning, either. But ACP and Sheldon heard it and marvel at my deafness.

I do get to watch the parade of hummingbirds. And early in the morning when the grass is still sodden with dew I can tell that the rabbits will soon be having their young and the place will be crawling with bunnies.

The big White Cochin is broody and we have set her with a motley clutch of eggs. There are some from Orphan Annie and some from the black hen and because Mel Belli is the father to them all and he is a Rhode Island Red, who knows what kind of chicks we shall have the third week in May?

It is a time for mating and hatching and all the other goings-on that have to do with renaissance in the woods and the only gripe a man can have is that it's all so darned interesting it cuts into the fishing.

Part Of The Good Life

Summer's Discordant Note

THE BEAR HUNTERS come to the hills with early summer and strike a discordant note with their big hound dogs and Southern-tinged accents.

Twenty years ago their kind were after the cougar, but now the bounty is gone and the cougars are thinned to a point where hunting them is poor sport.

The bear hunters stop by our cabin at River Place, looking for valuable hounds that have strayed from the hunt. "Those dogs are worth $400 apiece," says one of them, a beefy man with a trace of Oklahoma in his speech.

Not long afterwards one of the dogs slinks into the clearing and runs across the road where Snowbird's husband is pushing through a new trail with a bulldozer. One of the big logging trucks comes barrelling down the road and the driver hits his brakes, but as usual he is too late. The hound is smashed to pulp and there is nothing Jon can do but use the bulldozer to bury it well off the road. Each year the logging trucks claim their quota of deer and a half dozen dogs or so. The drivers often work under contract and seem always in a hurry to get the great logs to the hungry sawmills.

A FEW DAYS LATER A Certain Party is planting fir seedlings along the road and the fellow with the Okie accent stops by in his pick-up. There is a Latin tag on the side of his truck, "Ursus Horribilis," the scientific name for the grizzly. It is an inexplicable notation because the grizzly is long gone from these parts.

The hunter is looking for yet another of his dogs. One was reported stranded on a rock in the river for two or three days and even the sheriff's deputies were looking for it. A valuable hound gets as much attention as a missing child.

"Yes, there are lots of bear in those hills," says the hunter in answer to one of ACP's questions. What on earth, she wanted to know, do they do with them after they kill them?

"Well, I'm getting pretty tired of bear hamburgers," said the man. "I'm going to make some bear Thuringer."

ACP and I talk about it afterwards and wonder why the bears cannot be left alone. We hear nothing about them stealing lambs or other livestock. Apparently they do debark a few trees and that's why the lumber companies encourage the hunting. As long as there are men and hounds — and the bears to be hunted — such sport will continue.

I've often thought that the one animal that doesn't fit well into the ecological scheme is man. Because we keep chickens we must be on guard against predators such as weasel, chicken hawk, fox and bobcat. Because we grow flowers and a few vegetables, the moles must be destroyed.

Old Roy is good with the swallows and the rabbits, but quick to anger at their enemies. He doesn't like the cliff swallows because they are interlopers which fight with the barn and violet-green swallows. He resents the big owl that lives on Snowbird's acreage because he finds dead young rabbits on the path to the river and figures it to be the work of the owl.

Snowbird tells Roy he must not shoot the owl because it has its place in the scheme of things. She reasons that there are more rabbits than owls, which is doubtless correct. But then, if she had her way, nothing in nature would ever be trapped or gunned down.

New Neighbors
On Their Way

JON'S BULLDOZER is busy from early morning until late evening on the ridge. It is a friendly sound of summer because when he finishes his road he will be able to start his cabin and we will have another brace of good neighbors to look down on us.

The deer are plentiful again. Most of the fawns are dropped in June. A few are born in April and May, but wise Mother Nature knows that the cedar and salal are most luxuriant in June and provide the best lactation for the young deer. We see them on the road and frequently glimpse them swimming in the river.

It is a time now of the yellow finches, thick in the dewy morning grass. High in the trees we spot an occasional bright tanager. The mock orange is in flower and the banks of our river are afire with the foxglove with its healing digitalis. The first bandtail pigeons are heard on the hillsides and the grouse chicks, now feathered out, are almost tame at our approach.

Snowbird is gathering the last of the watercress near the falls for her salads and the strawberries are blood ripe. A Certain Party spikes the lamb with wild mint and the long summer days at River Place are like a book one cannot put down because it is such a joy. And when night finally comes we cannot wait for the morning light and Mel Belli's crowing because another day is there before us, misty with dew and pulsing with promises of new adventures.

The Excitement
Of September

THE ENTRIES in the diary I keep at the river cabin
are necessarily brief. "A dark, drizzly morning," reads
one for a day last week. "But a mild 58 degrees. Up
at 5:25 a.m. and not a glimmer of light until 6 a.m."

There's more. I mentioned watering the chickens while
the coffee perked and then going down to the river by
the first real light at 6:30. I even chronicled the covey
of mergansers which took flight as I neared the falls and
alluded to the water ouzel teetering on a rock where
I chose to clinch the first blob of salmon eggs on my
hook.

But a few lines in a diary cannot convey the excitement of such a morning. No words can quite describe
the quality of mist hanging on the slopes or the hint
of autumn that is something more than a few scrags
of maple leaf turning prematurely, well before the first
frost. Nowhere in my journal did I mention the thrill
of seeing the ducks wheel into the air and how I tried,
vainly, to count their exact number. And I did not jot
down the joy I felt at watching the ouzel do his water-
walk.

And if I were to try to keep a journal of all my moods
and fancies as I beat the rapids and pools with my fishing

line there would be precious little time for the fishing itself. And would it not be fatuous to try to capture in mere words the wonderment of a river one has come to love rather more than fatuously?

No, it is better to live such days than to write about them. It is better to fish for an hour or so with only Old Dog pacing her impatience on the bank and know that the Fisherperson is probably stirring and blinking into her first cup of coffee and pulling on her long wading boots and will presently be joining me in the canyon.

And then she comes shuffling down the steep path in her awkward boots and yellow slicker and sou'wester and I say, "Good morning, Fisherperson." In the city she is A Certain Party, but here we have a new private joke which grew somehow out of women's liberation and I am not sure she enjoys it as much as I do.

* * *

EARLIER IN THE WEEK it was vastly different. Old friends came from California, bringing four of their six children with them and the little cabin was crowded with sleeping bags and folding cots and small boys making their own batches of flapjacks with Himalayan blackberries picked near No Name Creek.

It was still very much summer then, with the mercury at 90 or better the day we came to River Place. Nell and Jim and their brood followed me down to the river that first warm evening and on the very first cast I picked up a bright summer steelhead near a red rock that I like to think only the fish and I know about.

It was a scant five-pounder, but a hen and quite lively. Jim scooped it up for me in the net and could not hide how impressed he was by Northwest fishing. I hadn't the heart to tell him it was the first time ever that I had caught a fish on the first cast.

Alas, we fished for the next three days with only a few small trout to show for our efforts. But the one steelhead was enough to provide dinner for all of us and Jim is the kind of guy who enjoys the fishing, fish or not. The days were all too short.

On the rainy last day of their visit we drifted the North Fork of the Lewis and all we got for our pains was a drenching. We forgot to bring the meats that day and we made our lunch of Camembert and Brie and slices of melon with a bit of smoked fish, but everyone had fun. In my diary at the cabin I wrote, "A good day." But it was something better than that.

All too soon our guests were on their way back to arid California and the cabin seemed terribly quiet and not a little lonely. Good friends do not wear at all thin in four or five days no matter what Ben Franklin had to say about visitors and fish "stinking" after three.

* * *

THE OTHER DAY the Fisherperson and I drifted the North Fork again. This time there was a good deal of water coming over the dam and the fish struck regularly. We took some nice cutthroat and the Fisherperson lost two big fish.

My friend Big Jim Conway was on the river in his jet sled and he gave us a tow back to the ramp several times, enabling us to make the drift more than once. Conway saw the Fisherperson lose her first big fish and then saw it jump several times. "It was a salmon," he said. "At least 12, maybe 14 pounds." Her six-pound leader didn't break, it just came untied from too much fishing.

An hour or so later a big steelhead hit the Fisherperson's new leader and she played it well until she got it next to the boat. However, as I went to net, it arched back into the air and wrapped a bit of slack line around its middle and threw the lure. I thought, for just a moment, that the stouthearted, liberated Fisherperson was going to do something feminine like cry, but she didn't.

Anyway, we went back to the cabin with wet bottoms and a nice catch of harvest trout and were content. That evening we were down at our own river again and saw millions of gnats swarming above the water with only a few bats to feed on them.

It was too dark to fish after 8 o'clock so we baked one of the bigger cutthroat and had him with lots of lemon juice and a bottle of Sancerre and I thought of Hemingway and how he would cool his bottles of Sancerre in the mountain streams when fishing in Spain, but surely he never had it any better than it was with us with our freshly caught harvest trout on one of the dying days of summer when there is just enough edge of sadness to temper what could otherwise be almost too good a day.

But that's what I wrote in the cabin journal before we turned in well before 10 o'clock. "A good day." What more could any man wish for himself or for his friends than just that?

Even A Visiting
Australian Gets
A Big Fish

Winter Again Grips The Woods

SINCE WINTER unsheathed its cutting edge a week ago we haven't been to that secret place where the river churns its way through the thick woods below our cabin.

But I know how it is. I have been there before when the cottonwoods and maples were newly naked after the first real frosts and the snow blanketed the thickets of alder below Snowbird Ridge.

My neighbor Charlie's place on the hill is visible above the winding river road now. In summer it was just a friendly flash of light glimpsed after dark. By day, screened by the heavy foliage along No Name Creek, it was all but hidden.

I can see the winter scene in my mind's eye. The icicles hang in heavy clumps along the road. More ice is forming in the quieter reaches of the stream and the waterfall is sluggish with heart-stopping beauty.

Everywhere there will be messages left by wild things on the snowy forest floor. I have more than memory to attest to that. The oldtimers have told me about the crimson stains left by the big cats after their encounters with deer and rabbits within shotgun pattern of our place. And just last Saturday my mother and brother were at the river to check on the plumbing and the chickens and they brought me back a tale they found written in the unbroken drifts.

Near the cabin my mother saw this "funny dog." It was, of course, a coyote driven down from the hills by winter hunger. My brother wondered if it had been after the chickens, but after reading the snow it was evident the coyote was after rabbits. Still, there is no denying that while the freeze lasts our little flock is in some danger.

* * *

GOOD NEIGHBORS do more than build good fences. Charlie has been a wonder since I was felled by my coronary and the snow came and the mercury dropped to near zero.

We were caught off guard, no doubt about that. Ordinarily I would have a light burning in the wellhouse to blunt the cold which penetrates the heavy insulation. But I never burn such a lamp before January. The same goes for "cracking" the taps in the cabin. Who ever heard of such precautions the first week in December?

When I came home from the hospital the second time I telephoned Mrs. Charlie with some trepidation. Were the pipes ruptured? Were the chickens dead with the cold? "You don't need to worry," said Mrs. Charlie. "That little old man has been down there and he's got the water running and your chickens are doing just fine."

That's the third person way Mrs. Charlie is wont to refer to Charlie. "That little old man" or, when she's feeling frivolous, that "fat little man." I wouldn't call Charlie either fat or little. He's just built a little closer to the ground than most of us.

Anyway, he went down to our place and thawed out the frozen pipes. And he put a bulb in the wellhouse and covered the outside taps and cracked those in the kitchen so the water would keep moving a little. He banked the chicken houses with straw and closed the

weasel proof doors and made sure that Hattie, our latest
tenant in the white house, was giving them some hot
water with their mash on freezing mornings. With such
good neighbors we have little about which to be concerned.

* * *

EARLIER THIS YEAR, after I had come home from
the hospital for the first time and both the telephone
and frequent visitors were becoming vexatious, we had
gone to the cabin for seclusion and quiet.

That was mid-November when the last leaves still
clung to the Gravensteins I had planted above the smokehouse and a few spawning salmon still lay dying in the
shallow riffles.

It was a restful time with nothing to do that really
needed doing. I stayed in bed late of a morning and
read at least a dozen books and wrote a little in my
journal. In the afternoon I went for little walks below
the ridge along the road where A Certain Party has been
setting out tiny hemlocks and a transplanted ponderosa
is doing extremely well.

I watched the game the squirrel played with our dogs.
Just a nubbin of a thing with an enormous bushy tail,
the squirrel would descend the trunk of a large fir about
75 feet from the cabin, coming down slowly and always
on the side of the trunk nearest the cabin so the dogs
would notice him. When he was three or four feet from
the ground the dogs would leap from the porch and
charge, the squirrel scampering back up the tree at their
approach. Frustrated, the dogs would go back to the
porch and then the game would begin all over again.
It lasted for more than an hour and after a few hours
respite it began again, the squirrel obviously enjoying
it more than the dogs.

Sometimes in the evenings I would bundle up in my
down jacket and long underwear and walk along the

edge of the woods. I remember the evening the moon
and stars were so bright and there was a big ring around
the moon, perfectly bisected by the contrail of a high-fly-
ing aircraft. A Certain Party is a firm believer in rings
around the moon forecasting rain and, sure enough, next
morning the rain began falling.

It was soon time to return to the city and the jangle
of the telephone and tedium of television. Then came
a return to hospital so they could take some pictures
of my clogged arteries. I was fretting to get back to River
Place again, but I was comforted by the knowledge that
Charlie, that good neighbor and "little old man," is keeping an eye on things. Not everybody is lucky enough
to have a Santa Claus for a winter caretaker.

The Best Cardiologist

FOR A LONG WHILE after I had my heart attack I was running scared, what the Spaniards call *un hombre muy timido*.

"It's only natural," said my cardiologist when I confided my fears to him. "After all, you have a death-causing disease."

I knew what he meant. We had talked about the chances of heart attack being 11 times greater for those who had had the first one than for those not yet members of the coronary club. At my insistence, he had quoted some actuarial tables which indicated I had 10 years, possibly more, possibly less, not the best odds for a man in his early 50's. After all, the arteriogram showed that one of the three arteries which served my heart was completely blocked, the other two partially stopped up with the crud of cholesterol.

Hence, I ran scared, taking some small comfort from a letter from a friend who said, "Lucky is the man for whom the bell tinkles before it tolls." That was the message. Time to shape up and eat right and live without anger and recharge the batteries whenever they showed signs of running down. I took it to heart, the pun intended and began living what I called the skim milk life, disdaining dairy products and fatty meats and the other rich things I had so much enjoyed. I lived on broccoli and mushrooms and chicken and cottage cheese, fruit juices, fish, tomatoes and onions.

I was a model patient. The doctor told me I could have two eggs per week, so I ate one. I gave up chopping wood and moving heavy furniture and refused to show my ire even in the most trying circumstances, keeping my cool. I went for long walks, but did nothing more strenuous. I dropped weight steadily, losing nearly 35 pounds in a matter of a few months. I gave up brandy and cigars. When I'd report for my physicals, my cardiologist would be immensely pleased.

Truth to tell, there were elements in my semi-invalidism which proved a boon. No longer did I have to fabricate excuses to avoid trying parties or boring meetings. My status as a "heart patient" with chronic atherosclerosis gave me a built-in rationale for dodging all irritants. People understood once they knew you had a ticker problem. Living without pressures was a lot easier because the pressures were considerably fewer.

On the other hand, there were things I missed. I missed rowing my drift boat, for example. I tried it cautiously a few times, but after a few hundred yards at the oars my arms would go dead with angina. I missed the pleasure of splitting wood for the fire and wondered how I would feed the stove in winters yet to come when the wood split for me by kind neighbors, as well as their kindliness, was exhausted.

Like all curious men who come to coronary occlusions in middle age, I did a lot of reading on the subject. Perhaps this is an unwise procedure. Inevitably we read articles about the wonders of by-pass surgery and other articles contending that surgeons are doing too many by-passes. Sooner or later we read of the Canadian doctors experimenting with Vitamin E and then we read elsewhere that the claims for Vitamin E have little validity. We encounter contradictory studies on the cholesterol theory. We read about the value of jogging programs and about the dangers inherent in jogging. With fascination, we peruse Norman Cousins' research on the value of laughter and other aspects of holistic medicine. And when we talk to our cardiologists about these things we have read we learn what we have already suspected, that medicine, for all of its progress and magical attributes, remains an inexact science.

Somehow, as the months go by and become years and we take our pills and face up to living with our tiny vials of nitroglycerine, we work it all out. In my case, it was a simple matter of getting to know my physiology better, to recognize the signs of fatigue and the irregular heart beat (atral fibrillation) that comes with stress. Because our main coronary arteries are congested, Nature develops the lesser, corollary arteries. I found myself able to do more and more. I began splitting wood again, cautiously at first, then for an hour or two at a time. While I continued to watch my diet, I began eating things I had been afraid to consume. I put on some of the weight I had lost, perhaps more of it than I should have, but people began telling me that I looked better and I did, less of a scarecrow. With my doctor's permission, I began enjoying an occasional cigar and a treasured bit of cheese. I'd have a glass of wine or two with dinner and, on rare occasions, a snifter of cognac. After a time, as my fears dissipated and my ability to do fairly hard work grew apace, I felt like at least a reasonable facsimile of my pre-coronary self.

Not long ago I mentioned all this to Dr. Donald Fisher, a family practitioner who had written an absorbing little book called, "I Know You Hurt, But There's Nothing To Bandage," and who had come to believe that illness is only rarely the result of the factors he had studied at medical school. He didn't seem at all surprised by my self-diagnosis of great improvement in both attitude and general health.

"You have that place at the river," he said. "I have an idea it's the best cardiologist you could have."

Mel Belli
And Company

LIKE TOPSY, the flock of chickens at our place on the river just growed.

It began with Mel Belli. The San Francisco lawyer celebrated his birthday in Portland and one of the gag gifts to him was a huge Rhode Island Red rooster, a fitting symbol of fertility.

The guests at the banquet were throwing morsels of food to the rooster and he was scared silly at all the attention. I caught him, clapped him in a cardboard box and told Belli I was going to take him to my country place. Mel thought it a good idea and, of course, we named the rooster for the "King of Torts." (It has proved an apt name. Our Mel Belli shows the same predilection for young ladies as does the lawyer, but that's another story.)

Once Mel Belli was ensconced as our alarm clock, I realized we had to get him some female companionship. I heard one of my neighbors in the city had half a dozen hens and was under pressure from his neighbors to be rid of them. We made a fast deal.

Everything went swimmingly with our small flock. The hens laid two, three, sometimes four or even five eggs a day. We gave them the run of the woods and

Fearsome Mel Belli II

they picked up a lot of bugs which somehow help them to lay big, heavy brown eggs with golden yolks and whites thick as molasses.

Mel Belli reigned like a tyrant over his six hens, but never forgot to wake us at the first glimmer of daylight. Along about 10 a.m. we'd hear a lot of cackling in the henhouse and we'd go down and find two or three eggs and poach them for a late breakfast.

But then things began to change. I had no sooner bought six New Hampshire chicks which I raised under a light bulb in the kitchen than someone gave us three more hens. A few weeks later I was in the village feed store and, on impulse, I bought six more chicks. About the same time our big Wyandotte hen went broody and we put eight eggs under her, resisting the urge to give her a full clutch.

Seven of the eggs hatched and our original flock of seven fowls became 29 of assorted shapes, sizes and colors. The small pen was now too small, so we had our neighbor, Charlie, build us a big chicken run. I doled out $50 for posts, lumber and chicken wire.

Then, a few weeks ago, my friend Van surprised us with eight Auracanas. They are beautiful birds with origins in Chile which lay "Easter eggs," i.e., eggs which come from the hen in bright colors.

It was immediately obvious that the established flock had no place in its pecking order for eight snooty aliens of South American lineage. They set upon the Auracanas, so we had to recruit Charlie once again, this time to build a second henhouse — a solid structure with a concrete floor to keep out the weasels and other varmits. I pungled up another $100 for lumber and concrete.

The Auracanas are happy with their new quarters. We let them out in the evenings to catch flying ants and to feed on the blackberries near the garden. Sometimes we have a sick hen and I talk to the poultry experts, but they all have different diagnoses. "Croup," says one. "Blocked crop," says another. A third talks of "coccidiosis." We discuss such things as the look of the stool. The Auracanas seem to be a fragile breed and we live in constant fear of losing them to some unnamed virus or other.

We have learned there is no profit in backyard chicken farming. When I go to the supermarket two things horrify me — the high price of beef and the ridiculously low price of eggs.

True, there is a vast difference between the small, white, insipid cold storage egg you find in the markets and the real eggs laid by our hens at River Place. But the days when a man could retire from a backbreaking factory job to his dream of a little chicken ranch in the country have gone glimmering like many another chimera in our crazy economy.

Small matter. I like chickens. I like fresh eggs. And I have a small, undernourished idea of some day raising an exotic breed more for show than for economic benefits.

At the moment, that idea can wait. I have eggs to gather and not one, but two henhouses to clean.

When The Sapsucker Comes

COUNTRY FOLK say it's best not to work the soil until it "scours," sometime in mid-April, but the soil near No Name Creek is sandy, friable, easily workable in March given a few sunny days.

At any rate, we have to try out the new toy. It's a new tractor which, we say, will pay for itself in a few years what with all the cutting of grass and plowing we're going to do with it.

Of course, we're kidding ourselves. The tractor won't save any money, but it will save a lot of work. We're not getting any younger and mowing a couple of acres of grass with a hand mower has lost its charm. So has handspading a big garden.

So Jon assembles the tiny tractor and attaches the tiller which is powered hydraulically and it is a marvelous machine. Jon goes charging about the big garden spot which hasn't been used for years and the soil comes pushing up from beneath the turf, black as anthracite and rich with promise.

One thing we learned from the start with a weekend home in the woods is that one job always leads to another. Now that we have the tractor we must have a shed in which to store it. It's time to clean out the old logging equipment shed.

River Place was once headquarters for a gyppo logging operation and for years rusting bits and pieces of logging machinery, choker cable, truck parts and other such detritus have been piling up in the shed. We begin pulling it out into the yard, separating the scrap iron from the scrap copper and brass. We make some unexpected finds such as a dozen cross-cut saw blades which bring $1 apiece from second-hand dealers and a giant old sharpening wheel which we'll probably keep as a conversation piece. Inevitably, we find boxes of blasting caps for dynamite, dangerous things to be handled gingerly.

* * *

THE RED-BREASTED SAPSUCKER is the first of the summer birds to return, coming like the daffodils, long before the swallow dares and when the breezes are still too nippy for the hummingbirds.

The sapsucker flies from the weeping willow to the smokehouse to the silver birch, sitting inexplicably on a wall of the smokehouse early in the morning, machine-gunning away against the galvanized iron and making a fearsome racket. The theory is that he's making all the noise to attract a mate which may well be the reason for it. There's no sleeping at River Place on such mornings anyway, so we don't mind the racket that much.

Spring is almost upon us and the signs of its coming are everywhere. The alder are tinged with scarlet blushes and the wild currants are pregnant with incipient blossom. The kitchen of our cabin is infested with miniscule ants which our neighbor, Charlie, calls "sugar ants." In the woods new ferns and tiny white flowers wait to welcome the springtime. Elephant garlic near the cabin pushes up in husky clumps. On the hill across the road we can hear the grouse, drumming their courtship music.

* * *

A CERTAIN PARTY likes to plant trees just for their

sheer esthetic or shade properties. Her proudest plantings are a clump silver birch, a blue spruce and a tall ponderosa. She gets almost as much pleasure just setting out prosaic firs and hemlocks.

To me, however, a tree should offer more than shade and beauty. I like trees which reward effort with blossoms and an eventual harvest. All my life I've wanted a small orchard and now, after two years of planting and pruning I feel I may one day achieve that goal.

I began with two Gravenstein apple trees, well-started saplings which are beginning their second spring not far from the cabin. To those, in the orchard proper, I added last year a Santa Rosa plum, a bing cherry, a Queen Anne cherry and a walnut tree.

Last fall I added a second walnut and at Christmastime a Bartlett pear, a gift from my sister. Still later I planted a second plum tree, two apricots and two peaches given me by a friend. Not long ago I added another pear. We have on order a chestnut and two winter-type apples which will give us 19 fruit and nut trees if we count the old peach tree already on the property which we are trying to nurse back to health after years of neglect. And now we have the new blueberry patch, filled with half a dozen varieties of four and three-year-old bushes and fenced against the deer and rabbits.

The sandy soil near the river seldom disappoints us. You simply stick a tree into it, prune it back a little and let sun and rain do the rest. So far we've kept spraying to a minimum. As the trees grow we'll probably have to do more dormant spraying, particularly of the peaches and apricots. The birds, too, will inevitably pose a problem. But right now all the little trees are oozing sap, buds and the promise of great bowls of fruit and huge kegs of cider to come. Surely, where there is so much new life a man can be forgiven for dreaming of bounty yet uncome.

The Business Of Fences

NOBODY LIKES the business of the fences, just as people rebel at the thought of locks.

So far, we have not fenced our little acreage on the river where the deer roam freely from woods to clearing. We see other places along the river which are virtual citadels surrounded by barbed wire on stout posts and festooned with No Trespassing signs. They do look forbidding.

The day may come when we shall have to fence the intruders out. Too many of them leave behind their luncheon wraps and other detritus and have small regard for the fishing laws. But we shall postpone such barriers as long as we can.

Meanwhile, we must stretch fencing of another kind. The young fruit trees in the orchard, for instance, have guards against the deer which dearly love to browse on tender saplings. The blueberry patch has its own chicken wire fence. Of course, if the deer are desperate to get at our blueberries they will easily leap a four-foot fence, but we're gambling that they won't be that hungry.

The garden is another matter. It is a big country-style garden which had not been used for seven or eight years and had gone back to grass and blackberry. With the wealth of manure from our chicken houses and the tractor it didn't take long to get it back into shape, but we had to have a fence unless it was to be a banquet table for the rabbits.

Hence, we tore down the old shed and salvaged from it a score of poles, each 21 feet long. Jon with his chain saw cut each of these into three seven-foot posts. After the posts were creosoted, Jon and Sheldon went to work with the posthole digger. Jon built "deadmen" for the corners and I went to town for more chickenwire and staples.

While we were stretching our counter-rabbit fence around the garden a neighbor from up river came along to say, "I hope you didn't buy that fence. If you call the game department and tell them the deer are in your garden, they'll fence it free. They'd rather do that than have people shooting the deer."

However, the deer have not been at our garden and it seems to me somehow a fraud to wait for it to happen just so we can save $50 on fencing. One of our problems nowadays is that we do too little for ourselves, ask too much of government.

I'm not sure that Robert Frost's dictum about good fences making good neighbors is always right. But good fences obviously make for better gardens, particularly in a clearing in the woods. I like having animals about the place, but I'm not going to be a gardener to them.

Literature
Vs. Turnip Culture

ESCAPISM is in fashion again and the bookstores bulge with wise and whimsical volumes about getting away from it all on tiny plots of land.

Of course, nowadays they don't call it "escapism." They invent other names for life away from the hurly-burly of the city. Ray Mungo, a recent defector from that celebrated commune with the winsome name of "Total Loss Farm" says the farm is an "outgrowth of fantasy-consciousness." The long established myth of making it on a few acres with a cow, a flock of leghorns and a wide garden is now called "psychic farming."

The old-fashioned idea of "escape" is good enough for me, fantasy or not. I never read that Depression era classic, "Five Acres and Independence," but I like to hew to the idea that it could be done if one had the fortitude to do it.

Many years ago the great book about the serenity of country life was David Grayson's "Adventures In Contentment," a best-seller of perhaps too genteel a mien for resurrection by today's communal denizens.

And not too many of the young people read Helen and Scott Nearing's "Living The Good Life." They do read "Total Loss Farm" and the other works inspired by that same commune where literary output and not turnip culture seems to provide the major source of income. So far there have been Alicia Laurel's "Living On The Earth" and Marty Jezer's "The Food Garden" as well as "Home Comfort," an anthology of essays by all the Total Lossers hoeing and typing (mostly typing) away up there in Vermont.

One of the contributors to the last-named compendium was a girl with the delightfully improbable name of "Verandah Porche." And it was a comment of hers that led a critic to fret that because of all the literary myth making going on up there in Vermont the reader is never quite sure what Total Loss Farm is really like.

* * *

WE ARE NOT into communal living at River Place unless you consider some sharing of things such as water, labor, eggs and favorite fishing holes as a communal lifestyle.

Snowbird and Jon have tapped into our well and we are happy that there is cold, pure water enough for all of us. Thanks to Jon's labors and our materials we have a new 20 by 30-foot workshop where two families can do their carpentering, welding and other fixing. We share the drift boat and many meals. But that is only because we are family and not because of any particular new or old philosophy.

However, I cannot but wonder if, like the communalists, I have been guilty of "fantasy-consciousness." Is my farming "psychic" or real? Do readers of these pieces have any sure idea of what River Place is like?

It could well be that in telling you of the delicate foxglove that grows along the paths that lead to the stream I have neglected to tell you just how many paths lead to the stream. And when I tell you that the violet-green swallows leave at 3 p.m. each day to swoop on insects below the falls, do I tell you of all the boxes full

of waiting young to which they return? They're small
matters, but indications that I have been remiss.

* * *

OUR WOODSY FARMLET, as I've mentioned before, embraces roughly five and one-half acres. Snowbird's ridge across the way is more than five times as
large and adds to an illusion that we are greater in
acreage than we are.

Happily, I have discovered the acreage lies almost exactly half in timber and half in clearing. The cleared
land offers ample space for the fruit and nut trees of
our orchard, the 17 shrubs in the blueberry patch, a
half-acre more or less of fenced garden and the chicken
coops and pens. The wooded land gives privacy, beauty
and perspective. It also shelters occasional squirrels,
grouse and other fauna.

Besides the coops and the new workshop, there is a
tractor shed, boatshed, well house, primitive smokehouse,
a small house occupied most of the time by tenant-care-
takers and our cabin.

Unlike the creative youngsters of Total Loss Farm,
we have almost no near neighbors. Except for Charlie's
place on the hill across the road, there are no houses
upstream for the best part of two miles. Downstream
there is nothing but woodland for better than a half-mile.

Those then are the bare outlines of River Place. I could
tell you that our upstream boundary is a nameless creek
which we have taken to calling No Name Creek and
that our downstream property line follows a long-disused
logging road. But you would not get the feel of the an-
cient log bridge from that, now but a jackstraw tumble
of decaying logs. I could mention the four paths leading
through the woods to the better fishing spots along the
river, but it would be difficult to delineate for you the
tangled vines and brush that threaten them or the gla-
mor they assume in June with the budding foxglove.

I might allude to the jungle of blackberries behind the chicken coops, but you would see that as evidence of unkempt land and miss the taste of their August ripeness. If I were to describe the stretches of fishable water as best I could, it would not quite be like wading them with fly or spinning rod in one hand, walking staff in the other. And I know all too well that no matter how much I told you of the garden where tomatoes, corn, peppers, beans, snow peas, cucumbers and squash yearn for the July sun you would think me guilty of "psychic farming" when I attempted to describe the richness of that black and fine-as-talcum soil.

In short, the urge of writer to fantasize about life in his particular Eden may be resisted, but the need of the reader to build the same fantasy-consciousness is omnipresent. It is because nearly all of us have the urge to flee the urban pavements — at least occasionally — that we build our own castles of escape literature with only the tiniest nudge from the original architects.

No, we have no delusions about independence on our scant five acres. Even if we took to eating roots and berries and poaching deer like our pioneer ancestors, we could not hack out a paycheckless existence in such a milieu. We have neither the strength nor the expertise for such a venture.

The idyll of River Place, at least for a time, must remain an occasional idyll, a temporary escape from reality held at arm's length only for a few hours at a time, largely because we would not bar that reality from our lives forever, even if we could. The charms of woodlot, river and farmlet are, like the headier wines, best savored in moderation. Taken daily they might not pall, but then they very well could. Such an approach, it seems to us, will save us from the charge, if not the dangers, of indulging in "fantasy-consciousness."

The
First
Addition

July Casts Its Spell

WE RISE EARLY these mid-July days because there is much to be done and the afternoon sun glazes the garden and orchard with a varnish of heat.

The first one out of bed puts the coffeepot on the burner and turns the chickens out of their houses in a scramble for the morning ration of corn.

We linger over the first coffee and talk of the watering and weeding to be done, but the thought that a steelhead may have moved into one of our fishing holes during the night keeps us from any real breakfast until that possibility has been investigated. A Certain Party baits her hook with tempting nightcrawlers. Jon stays true to his fly rod and an assortment of red flies. I tend to stick to my brass wobblers.

As I work downstream, exploring the various patches of likely water, I see A Certain Party fishing her favorite hole below the falls where a mallard hen, nearly hidden in the overhanging alder along the bank, is raising a fearful racket. She has 12 newly-hatched ducklings, six in bright yellow, six in downy black. It's the big dog, Salah, that upsets her so. Salah wouldn't hurt her or her charges, but she doesn't know that and betrays her presence with all that quacking.

After 20 minutes I'm convinced the fish are still down river and I go back to the cabin to make my breakfast. By the time I've sliced the ham and mixed my batter the others are back from the river, pulling off their boots and putting away their gear. It's time for summer's chores.

* * *

MID-JULY'S GARDEN is a wondrous thing. The rows of corn, planted at weekly intervals, are of varying stature. The first planting ranges from three to four feet and the bantam varieties, although much shorter, are already forming ears.

The potatoes, carefully tilled and hilled by my Australian father-in-law, are bushes of brightest green and the pole beans, climbing against the chicken coops, grow as though being chased by demons. We've been picking the snow peas for a fortnight and they've been so popular there just aren't enough for freezing. The cucumbers are beginning to blossom and the tomato vines are heavy with green fruit.

The well has lived up to our best hopes for it. We keep sprinklers going in the garden, in the orchard and on the blueberries and always seem to have enough water. If we were still dependant on the spring we'd be desperate for it, but the deep, drilled well seems to have tapped an underground river.

There are a few problems in the orchard — sick pear trees and a dying walnut. And we were premature in taking down the tree guards. The deer haven't worried the trees, but the rabbits have been gnawing at peach and apricot. Jon and I repair the damage and erect new guards.

* * *

FOUR BROODING HENS have given us a new batch of chickens. They are seemingly everywhere, busy balls of fluff scratching for worms and learning the facts of life under tutelage of the hens.

The old hens, of course, aren't laying nearly so well in the hot weather. In May our 20 hens were still giving us 15 to 17 eggs per diem. Now we're lucky to get 10 eggs each day, more than enough for our wants. Snowbird has acquired four domestic mallards which have become the farmyard comedians, their antics fun to watch.

But the best show in the hollow is at our neighbor Charlie's place where his bantams live wild in the woods behind his house, hiding their clutches of eggs in the thickets and producing an endless round of chicks. At night the tall firs are studded with bantams which roost 10, 15 or even 20 feet above the ground, trying to keep out of reach of nocturnal predators.

*   *   *

WHEN THE GARDEN is weeded and watered and the chickenhouses have been cleaned we sit under the twin cedars by the cabin sipping glasses of tonic water and lime juice.

If there are four or more of us we play desultory bridge. If even that proves too tiring in the heat we wander down to the river to watch the ducks and leaping trout and cool off.

In the evening as it grows cooler we put a chunk of fish or a meat loaf in the oven and chill a bottle of wine. We sit for a long time over dinner, watching the moon rise above the hemlocks to dust the canyon with its silvery rays. No matter how hot the days it is always cool enough to sleep well on the river at night.

With the moon so beautiful and the cool night air so soft we stay up late, but not too late. In the morning we not only have to catch the best part of the summer day, but nurse again the hope that it will be the day on which one of us catches the greatest steelhead ever to rest for a time in one of those shining pools below River Place.

The Snowbird
Helps Set Out
The Apple Trees

Agreeable Books,
Women And Rivers

"AFTER A GOOD WOMAN and a good book,"
wrote Robert Louis Stevenson, "there is nothing so agreeable on earth as a good river."

Since I found that quotation, I've tried it on friends
who are unimpressed. They're city folk, of course, people
who thrive on the bright lights of the metropolis.

However, there are, indeed, few things quite so agreeable as a good river, particularly in August. August
means low water and the city low water tires easily because it has so much more work to do.

We ask little of our river here in late summer. If it
be but sweet and pure and strong enough to carry the
fish and quench the thirsts of those creatures that drink
from it, it is enough. We don't ask it to generate electrical
power nor to carry ships nor to process wood pulp or
cannery produce nor even to float our drift boat which
my Aussie father-in-law is giving a fresh coat of paint
now that the river is too low for drifting.

It has been a dry summer and we see rocks rising above
the surface we have not seen before, at least not in August. I remember wading the river at this time last year
and having to swim part way where there is a channel
a bit deeper than a man is high. But this year Charlie's

grandson, Casey, wades it easily, plowing across the rapids in his tennis shoes and jeans and emerging awash with sand and strands of moss on the far bank.

A shallower river, of course, means a narrower fishway and A Certain Party is teaching us all a thing or two about steelheading. Each of the past four weekends she has landed a big fish — three of them good-sized steelhead and the fourth a 16-inch harvest trout, the delicate flesh of which makes a gourmet prize.

ACP is a worm fisherperson and that means she has to have a lot of worms, not easy to find in the dry months. Even Charlie's usually inexhaustible supply of nightcrawlers seems badly depleted. Hence, Casey helps ACP water our lawn and the two of them pick worms late into the night while we lesser fishermen go to bed with good books.

*   *   *

IT'S BLACKBERRY TIME at River Place and that means picking enough for pies and jam while cursing the nettles that thrive among the vines. They're sugar sweet this year, as black as telephones and bursting with goodness. After ACP and Snowbird make their jam they get out a "secret recipe" from a Jewish friend for a dill pickle that needs no alum, no vinegar, just a lot of spicy things like red peppers, dill weed and tiny onions. Never do we set so bountiful a table as we do in August when summer is at its ripest.

For breakfast we have blueberry pancakes with blackberry syrup and newlaid eggs, all provided at least in part by our farmlet. Dinner last night was a feast. ACP filleted her latest steelhead and it came from under the broiler a marvelous peach colored piece de resistance garnished with wedges of lemon. Earlier in the day I had put down a batch of bread and the loaves were still warm from the oven when the fish went under the broiler. From the garden came freshly-picked chard and new, sweet onions. Mrs. Charlie sent down a pot of green beans from the hill, succulent with bacon bits and there were also slicer cucumbers with vinegar and onion and a panful of potatoes O'Brien. I iced a tall green bottle of Pinot Chardonnay which proved a satisfying obbligato to a meal otherwise orchestrated from nature's larder.

No matter how busy we are with fowls and garden, we always make time for the river. Sometimes we don't bother to take our rods but just go down to the pools below the woods and watch the clear waters thread through the red boulders where the herons scavenge for breakfast and the ouzels make sport with spray and rivulet. It takes a lot of study at all times of the year to get to know a river just as it takes time and effort to know truly a good woman or a good book. The better you get to know any of the three, the more agreeable they tend to become.

**Horseshoes Champ
Of Cutthroat
Hollow**

"No Bandicooting Allowed"

THERE'S A NEW SIGN at the garden gate printed in crude red letters. Visitors to River Place don't understand the sign and the dictionary would be of no help to them. It says simply, "No Bandicooting Allowed."

True, a big dictionary will tell you that a bandicoot is an Australian marsupial of nocturnal habits not unlike a possum. But that same dictionary fails to mention that as a verb form it's Australian slang for "fossick" or "scratch around" and that to bandicoot is usually to dig around the potato plants at the surface, gleaning the tiny new potatoes without disturbing the deep-lying spuds.

A Certain Party is an incurable bandicooter. She dotes on new potatoes and is as profligate as I am provident. She reasons that the tiny surface potatoes won't grow much larger anyway and should be eaten at the peak of flavor. Her argument has the force of logic and the sign is naught but a rearguard action to stem the unstemmable.

Early September is the bottom line for the weekend gardener. Suddenly all the weeding and watering and mulching is all worthwhile as the harvest comes to table and freezer.

Each evening now we have ears of sweet corn just picked before it is popped into the boiling water. Snowbird pops the ears into the pot while Jon keeps an eye on the sweep-second hand of his watch. You've all known three-minute egg faddists: Jon is a three-minute corn faddist.

Besides the corn there are bandicooted potatoes, vine-ripened tomatoes and string beans, both green and yellow. There's blackberry cobbler made from the last of the Evergreens. Now and then we have one of our few green peppers or open a "green" jar of the still fermenting pickles, just to sample them.

* * *

WE HAVE A NEW HEN and while it provides no eggs, it provides a lot of fascination. It's what is known as a "transparent hen" and what it is is one of those glass-walled incubators made for grade children to watch the hatching of chicks.

Our roosters operate on a hit and miss basis so 10 of the first 19 eggs we put into the incubator proved infertile. But from the other nine we had eight chicks, six of which are now strong enough to brave the rigors of the chickenyard.

After some deliberation we gave the six chicks to Spooky. Spooky is a black Monarchi hen which, until nine weeks ago, was afraid of her own shadow. She then went broody and sat on a nest for eight weeks, attacking anyone who came near her but systematically smashing three different clutches of eggs. She seemed a total loss as a mother, but she took the incubator chicks and made them her own with a fierce acceptance. With hens like Spooky we don't need a mechanical brooder.

More interesting than the Labor Day hatching of the chickens was the later hatching of quail eggs. Unlike chicks, the tiny quail come from the egg as though being born was a workaday occurrence. Within a half hour or less they stitch their ways around the miniature eggs, cutting them into two perfect hemispheres. In a few hours they are dry and a few hours after that they begin taking water and food and utter loud cheeps. They are as small and pretty as Christmas walnuts but striped like pocket gophers. We're told the females will lay in six weeks, these Japanese quail having somewhat the same characteristics of breeding as rabbits. If we can learn to eat the eggs as they do in Japan where they're considered a treat, we'll have a new delicacy for the table.

There is a new chill in the air these evenings and a trace of frost in the mornings. The garden will soon be a withered place for the fowls to scratch, but we're not hurrying summer on its way. We need another three weeks of summer if the garden is to pay a full dividend.

And yet, the pattern is there, discernible for anyone with an eye on the woods to see. To everything there is, indeed, a season. It matters little if the cabbages don't ripen and the chickens get the half-formed heads just as they'll get the corn which doesn't mature. The rains will come and fill the river again so the salmon can make their pilgrimages to the gravel beds. And we shall survive the winter even if we have only 50 quarts of kosher pickles, though it will mean real hardship.

The Need For Dying

OUR NEIGHBOR CHARLIE can't understand people who have trouble killing and dressing meat for the table. Of course, Charlie was born and reared on a farm and is untainted by the squeamishness of more sophisticated folk.

The city dweller has long since lost touch with the realities of butchering. To him, a chicken is something that comes plucked, drawn, quartered and neatly tucked in its cellophane package. A piece of steak is a sculpted work of art trimmed with parsley in a showcase. Lamb chops somehow grow on trees, I suppose, already dressed in those little paper booties meatcutters call "frills."

There is something detached, unreal about the maiden lady who couldn't possibly kill anything, gets upset over the hunters who slay upland birds or deer, but sits down two or three evenings a week to a medium rare sirloin. Not that such surrealism knows any gender. Some of the burliest and most masculine of men couldn't clean a trout, let alone butcher a hog. The very thought of such activity will make some men blench. As America grows more and more urban, it breeds more and more sissies.

AT RIVER PLACE we have learned that just as spring brings new life, the autumn brings a time when other things must die.

Summer's proud garden takes on a sad bedraggled look with the arrival of October's rains and the first knife edge of frost. We leave the undeveloped ears of corn on the stalks, hoping that they may yet fill out a little, but it is a forlorn hope. The cucumber vines yellow and wilt and the beans, after four pickings, are now but dying seed pods. We pull half a dozen of the tomato vines out by the roots and hang them over the rafters in the machine shop, but most of the green fruit rots before it ripens. We don't worry about things that form under the earth. The potatoes are secure for another month or so and we still harvest a bunch of carrots now and then to go with the hardy squash.

Nothing is wasted from the garden. The corn stalks will go to a neighbor's cows several miles down the river. The rotting tomatoes and poor ears of corn go to the always hungry chickens. Those cabbage plants we set out too late in the season will become mulch. The compost pile will grow all winter long, enriched by the litter from the henhouses and the duck pen. Locked in all the decay of the garden is the promise of next year's fertility.

But death is everywhere in October. The hunters move up and down the river road in their jeeps and pickups, bristling with the urge to kill. They are looking for deer now and later will probe the high country for elk. When the big game is scarce they sometimes blaze at the grouse in brush patches near the road. Early in the morning the sound of gunfire echoes through the canyon and one of Snowbird's dogs, gun shy since a pup, hides under our tractor shed, refusing to come out.

* * *

IT IS TIME NOW to cull the chicken flock. All summer long the hens have brooded by fits and starts, hatching their clutches of eggs.

The young pullets, naturally, are spared. They will begin their laying this winter and that biological potential spares them the axe. But there are always young roosters and once they reach their growth there is no point in keeping them, not with scratch at more than $10 a hundredweight.

Neither Jon nor I relish the job of slaughtering chickens. Jon used to do it on his uncle's farm. "I didn't like it then and I don't like it now," he says. I used to help my German grandfather singe the plucked birds with flaming newspaper when I was very small and I've cleaned a lot of birds since. I can't say that I enjoy it. It's just one of those chores which has to be done.

Charlie usually kills a chicken or two when he's expecting company for dinner. Jon and I would rather get the job done all at once. We round up all the roosters, tie their legs with binder twine and dispatch them, one after another, with quick blows from a sharp axe. We dunk them briefly in buckets of scalding water to loosen their feathers and then pluck them behind the shed, saving some of the colored plumage for trout flies. The gizzards we save for Charlie. We don't singe the birds with burning newspapers, but with a little propane torch from the shop.

We work at it for two hours and when we are finished we have a pile of chickens ready for the freezer. They will be a lot tastier than those 8-week wonders they fatten with chemicals for the supermarkets.

The job done, we wash up and then walk down to the river to watch the Chinook spawning in the gravel beds, great gaunt creatures about to die. A Certain Party is always a little sad watching them in their death throes, but I feel no real compassion for them. Surely the salmon knows that October is a time for the killing and the dying that means not an end to life but ever new beginnings.

Of Jadeite Water
And Oak Tables

OUR TUMBLING RIVER is not so grand as the Columbia, not so wide as the Deschutes, not as wild as the Rogue nor as picturesque as the Metolius. In a region laced with mountain streams and all their attendant calendar scenery it makes but a fair-to-middling show most of the year.

And yet in November it is surely one of the loveliest rivers you will find the world over. The autumn rains and first snows cleanse its banks and fill its empty tributaries and it puts on winter fat like a force-fed goose.

There are times when rain roils its waters, but the turbidity goes once the weather clears for a day or two. It is then that it wears its best finery.

"It's like jade," says A Certain Party. "Not Chinese jade, but Wyoming jade, the mineral they call jadeite."

And so it is, with a surface translucence which ends about a foot below the velvety depths which hide the mysteries of migrating fish, otter and beaver.

The jadeite waters are dappled with the gold of vine maple and when we drift for steelhead and cutthroat the leaves keep fouling the lines. But each time we are forced to reel in and clear the hooks it is but another excuse to slow the boat and drink a little more deeply of a seasonal elixir as heady as hard cider. The travel writers extol the beauties of fall color in New England I suspect only because they have not seen what autumn does to our woods. And perhaps it is best that they continue in their ignorance.

* * *

NOVEMBER'S WET SNOW accompanies a chill which mocks those warm days we had in October. As the great moist flakes tumble down we huddle in the cabin around the scarred oak table.

The circular oak table is the base of foul weather activity. It is a rather interesting table, at least it has an interesting history. For years it served in one of Portland's after-hours gambling joints. I ran across it in the long empty premises one day and it was covered with both a layer of green felt and a patina of dust. I made the man who owned the property an offer for it and he told me to take it, he no longer had any use for it.

Stripped of its grimy felt and with most of the cigarette burns repaired, it is a reasonably good table. Nothing fancy, mind you, but solid and conducive to friendly dining. The Chinese always use round tables for formal dining and they know more about food and the serving of it than anybody.

My neighbor, Charlie, casts acquisitive looks at my table. One week he'll offer me $25 for it, the next $35. Once he went all the way to $37.50. I have no interest in selling it. Not only is it a good table for a cabin, but I like to fantasize about its history. How many royal flushes did it see in all those years of poker games? How much money was stacked on it? What prominent citizens once sat around it, drawing to open end straights? It is a table that has known hard use and one sturdy enough to serve at least a century more.

It is at the old table that I fill out the cabin diary. It is there on Sunday mornings that I knead the dough for my bread. We eat all our cold weather meals on it and in the evenings we use it to play kitchen bridge or any of a dozen word games. But often we just sit there watching the birds scrabbling in the brush under the cedars or the squirrels scrambling up the hemlocks. Oak tables are great for just sitting now that summer is long gone and the charms of River Place are the quieter moments when the loudest sounds are rustle of dry leaf or sudden whir of wings in the muted breeze above the flowing jade.

"What's New?"

EVERYWHERE when men meet they seek out the news. Even the Malay in his jungle greets another Malay with "Apa khabar?," a reasonably approximate version of the "What's new?" I put to Charlie when we reach the river.

Charlie and Mrs. Charlie always have a budget of tales for us. They know each rock and mud slide on the river road and just how many trucks and cars have gone into the ditch. They know when a boat capsizes in the rapids and when an airplane crashes in the wilderness country above the headwaters.

"What's new?" I ask Charlie and then I sit back and Mrs. Charlie proceeds to tell me with occasional interruptions from her husband. Charlie can't get many words in when he's at home, but he does like a story to be well told.

Always, interspersed between the more routine happenings, are the classic yarns. Mrs. Charlie will spend 15 minutes telling you how a grocer in town cheated her and why he's lost her business forever and then suddenly drop a gem.

The other day Mrs. Charlie was telling us about an early settler on the river, an octogenarian who's had a rough time of it lately. Without any pause she happened to mention Nelson's pigs. "Can you imagine a man feeding pigs like that?" she asked. Like what, I wondered aloud. I knew Nelson was a man with a farm a couple of miles up the road.

"Why, he'd just feed them and feed them," said Mrs. Charlie. "He'd pick up boxes of garbage for them in the restaurants and supermarkets and then when he got home he'd let them have it all. They got so fat they had to eat sitting down and then they got even fatter and they could only lie there."

"Had to butcher 'em," said Charlie. "They only dressed out to 70 or 80 pounds. You can't overfeed a hog."

A million stories in the naked city? There are ten times that many in the country. And most of 'em a lot more interesting.

March Stirs Thoughts Of Plowing

BLUSTERY MARCH swaggers a lot, but there's rarely any real meanness in him. He's more like an itinerant peddler with a gypsy knapsack, taking from it all kinds of things from snow to sap-pushing sunshine.

Last week the sun shone most of two days and lordie, lordie it was good. The fowls had their first dust baths in many weeks and the ducks splashed in their wading pool while the dogs lazed under the still bare willow.

After years at River Place we know a false spring when we see one. The alder thickets on Snowbird's hill are already tipped with that pink tracery that comes before the budding, but the evening chill and morning frost are still much with us.

We've seen a band of grosbeaks in the grass near No Name Creek and the budding lilac and blooming crocus suggest that spring may be at hand. But the flurries of snow and ice remind us that winter dies hard. Even the swallows, one of the earliest harbingers of spring, are yet at least a fortnight away.

* * *

IT WAS NEARLY two weeks ago that Charlie, on his way to butcher some chickens and carrying a bucket of scalding water, slipped on a wet plank and fell with the water, filling one of his rubber boots and suffering third-degree burns.

He's a tough old coot and has survived a dozen accidents which have claimed lesser men. He's been bitten by rattlesnakes and burned by high-voltage electricity and once had his ears nearly torn from his head in a savage auto accident. At first it looked as though he would take the burnt leg in his stride, but after a night of pain he went to hospital. He stayed four days and then came home where Mrs. Charlie kept applying wet compresses to his seared leg.

After a few days of agony at home it was obvious that Charlie's burns were infected. I drove him back to town and hospital in my little truck and he waxed sentimental. "I don't know what a man would do without his neighbors," he said. He remains in hospital, his neighbors feeding his hogs and helping Mrs. Charlie to keep up her supply of firewood. Good neighbors do a lot more than build good fences.

Blustery, rainy March is a time when the ducks lay but do not yet nest, when A Certain Party's umbrella frightens our quail and the river runs too swift for all but the most zealous fishermen. It is a time, however, to set the incubator with eggs and sow the tomato and cabbage seeds. April plowing is only a month away and the black, rich earth of River Place will soon warm to match our fever of expectancy.

So That's A Grosbeak?

NOT LONG AGO I reported seeing a flock of "orioles" by No Name Creek. Now, I make no claims to expertise when it comes to bird identification. My friend Tom McAllister, who is an expert ornithologist, chides me for the "oriole" report.

But I really catch it from John B. Crowell, Jr., general counsel for the Louisiana-Pacific Corp. and a bird-watcher himself. When I wrote about the "orioles" in my newspaper column he sent me a devastating letter in which he made the following points:

(1) Orioles almost never travel in flocks.

(2) Orioles would rarely be seen even singly on the ground.

(3) Scott's Oriole is limited to the Southwest and has never been recorded in Oregon or Washington.

(4) Bullock's Oriole (now lumped with the Eastern Baltimore Oriole and both called Northern Oriole) does not arrive in the Northwest until May.

(5) It is very probable that my visitors were Evening Grosbeaks — a nice bird to have around.

I'm learning — the hard way.

Pekins Gotta Walk,
Mallards Gotta Fly

Weathering The Rain

THE SPRING RAIN breeds indolence. Without the usual May sunshine the garden tends to stagnate and so do the gardeners.

I don't mean that we just sit around and whittle or play with that whittler's contrivance known as a gee-haw whimseydiddle. We fish a little, pull a few weeds and even do a little painting, but our hearts aren't in it.

We worry about the ducks because they've taken to crossing the road. A log truck hit one of the mallard drakes and I found him in the ditch, badly mangled. Now that the hen mallard has her brood of little ducks it's time I finished the fence. We've already lost some of the ducklings, but there is no way to watch them all the time. There were 16 eggs in the nest she made in the ferns and 13 hatched, only one of them a cripple. The cripple went first. A few days later the 12 were 11 and a few days after that the 11 were 10. Maybe its a weasel or a raccoon that gets them. Anyway, we now lock them in a pen each night.

The business of the 20 young Rhode Island chicks was something else. It must have been the work of stray killer dogs, but there's no way of knowing for sure. Something broke into their pen and took all 20 leaving not a trace, not a feather. They were all sexed pullets getting on for five weeks, timed to take over for the laying hens during the next molt.

Because of power failures and malfunctions, we've also had trouble with the incubators this year, losing pheasant and quail eggs. Now we have eggs under three broody hens, hoping they'll serve better than the fractious incubators. What with the rain and the slow garden and the loss of the birds it's been a bad May for us.

* * *

MRS. CHARLIE bought a pregnant burro the other day, spent all her babysitting money on it.

"It cost me $65, but it's worth it to me," she said. "That little old man is just getting too old to swing that scythe."

Mr. and Mrs. Charlie have had burros before and found them efficient lawnmowers. Their front "lawn" is really a fenced-in pasture and the weeds and grass grow waist high if something doesn't keep it down.

When we first came to River Place Charlie had two burros. They were friendly animals, but noisy. The new burro, Jennie, is even noisier.

"She sounds just like a foghorn," says Snowbird. She remembers lying in bed as a small girl listening to the ships sounding fog warnings on the river, a city sound.

I don't mind the braying, but Charlie's peacock does make a lot of racket. Between the burro and the peacock River Place isn't as quiet this year. However, the sounds are all friendly ones and once the dark comes there is only the croak of the frogs and the endless rush of the river.

All things considered, troubles and rain not excepted, the country still has charms which beggar those of the city. We know that the sun will come after the rain.

Leveling With The Land

THE MOST USEFUL tool at River Place is the carpenter's level. Sure, the axe and chain saw come in for a lot of use, as do the rake and the hoe. But there's nothing more utilitarian in unlevel country than a good level.

I grew up in a river valley in South Dakota that's said to be the most level stretch of ground on earth. Here we're faced with abrupt ridges, precipitous cliffs, undulating meadows and gentle wooded slopes.

Charlie showed up the other day while I was building a run for the baby pheasants and looking for a place to put it. The books say to put young pheasants on grass and my run is a long, bottomless cage. The idea is to set it on level grass and move it each week or so.

"You won't find any level ground around here," said Charlie. "You won't find any anywhere along the river." Charlie should know. He's built houses and cabins and henhouses and pigpens up and down the river for years. He used to do a lot of building for a fellow who operated a "fat farm" for chunky girls on the upper river, an enterprise that went broke despite the plentitude of overweight young ladies who came to endure scanty meals, hiking trails and long hours of horseback riding.

Our two or three acres of cleared land look level enough to the eye, but a long carpenter's level betrays the slant no matter where we build.

Hence, the pheasant run is propped up with rocks on one side. If the pheasants manage to escape, it doesn't matter overly much. Sooner or later they'll be released to make it on their own in any instance.

* * *

THE ACREAGE we now call River Place was once known as "Cutthroat Hollow" and Mrs. Charlie likes to tell us it was either because someone once cut his throat there or had his throat cut there. But real old-timers on the river say that isn't the case at all. The less macabre explanation is that the river at one time abounded in cutthroat or harvest trout in this particular stretch.

If one must have the macabre as part of folklore, there is another well-attested story told by Mrs. Charlie that will suffice. It concerns the woman with a hydrocephalic child who, after years of enduring remarks about her offspring, took an axe to it. But even that was 50 years ago and on quite another part of the river.

The problems of River Place are not the problems of the city. It's coming to grips with the hard fact that 16 ducks never stop eating. It's burying the dead hens in the garden and nursing the Granny Smith apple tree through a siege of blight. It's wondering if the old dog will come through her bout of bronchitis with the vet's help. "It'll be touch and go for her," said the vet. "She's got her age against her."

We have some friends who moved from the city to the country not long ago. An aunt told them, "You won't like the farm. It's just death, death everywhere." They have lost a lot of their calves to disease, but are not discouraged.

It's true enough that on the land you find death and

often it seems to overwhelm you. But there is also more life to be found in the woods or on the farm, and dying is part and parcel of all that living. It's a truth as simple as the bubble on my carpenter's level and no need being morbid about it.

Is Longevity Overrated?

SUMMER BRINGS more visitors each year as friends and relatives come to share a small part of the contentment we find in our woodsy idyll.

Some of the visitors are scheduled, some not. It matters little except when there are chores to be done and a bothersome guest insists on hours of chattering small talk. When that happens we contrive escapes to garden or shop. leaving Miss Loquacious or Mr. Yak-yak to laze in the sun. After a few days they get the hint and cut their sojourns short, moving on to more tolerant households.

For the most part, the visitors are a joy. Last week Jim and Nell were back again, this time leaving their sizable brood behind them in California's San Joaquin Valley. Jim is the only friend left from my boyhood days on the Middle Western prairie whose valued acquaintance I've been able to nurture for the best part of half a century. Nell, the rosy cheeked daughter of Dutch dairy farmers, is as friendly and amiable as an Edam cheese and no trouble at all. Their visits to River Place are too few and all too short.

Jim and I, as old friends will, talk not only of cabbages and sealking wax, but of far more important things. We dwell a lot on the meaning of our lives and the patterns they have taken. We wax nostalgic for lost loves and vanished ambitions, but never for too long, because we are both men whom life has treated with modicum of luck and great dollops of affection. Jim is a successful presthodontist whose busy practice finds him ministering to accident and cancer victims whose jaws have been ravaged by either mishap or disease. I make my living writing about people for a newspaper. Jim is interested in my work and I in his. Talk, for us, comes easily and while our women may occasionally tire of our endless sessions, we keep at it, knowing that our next chance will be a year or two away.

Last week we talked a lot about two disparate things. One of those was Costa Rica, a country which Jim and Nell came to know only when one of their sons married a Costa Rican girl two or three years ago. They have since made five or six trips to that Central American country and are great admirers of it. Jim points out that it is the only nation in the world without a standing army. Nell extols the beauties of the climate and the friendliness of the populace. I have a certain curiosity about it and we discussed at length the possibilities of our accompanying them on one of their trips there in the future.

We also talked lengthily about dying, a subject of particular interest to Jim because he has seen so many of his cancer patients wrestle with the realities of their mortality. Although I believe we both have healthy attitudes about the temporal nature of life, my enthusiasm for the topic waned after an hour or two. Like most Americans of my generation and European cultural background, I find macabre matters somewhat depressing. Jim had recently attended a lecture by Dr. Elisabeth Kubla-Ross, an authority on death and dying, and was entranced by her naturalistic approach.

All too soon, their stay was over and they drove eastwards, planning to visit our old hometown before returning to California. We bid our adieux and went back to our gardening and fishing, thinking how grand their visit had been and wondering a little if we would ever be able to afford a trip with them to Costa Rica.

Early the next morning the telephone rang. (We finally succumbed to installing one, but fiercely keep the unlisted number from all but our closest friends.) It was Jim, telephoning from Lewiston, Idaho where they had spent the night in a motel.

"I couldn't sleep," said Jim. "I have the most wonderful idea. You and I are going to do a book about dying. I'm convinced the time is ripe for it. We'll go to Costa Rica and put the whole thing together in a few weeks. It's a great place to work. I've already got all the ideas. I just need you to put them into words."

A bit taken aback by his fervor, I asked him to elaborate on his idea. He immediately launched into a chapter outline. There would be a chapter on wills and bequests and other matters incidental to estate planning. There would be a chapter on how to give a great party before one's death, detailing the do's and don'ts of such a gathering. There would even be a chapter discussing easy ways of dying through the use of certain drugs.

The last suggestion startled me. I reminded Jim that there were state laws about taking one's own life and that what he was contemplating sounded perilously close to a "how to" suicide manual. He didn't see it quite that way and went on for an hour, running up a staggering long distance bill, as he elaborated on his theme.

Finally, I told him I would have to think on it. I had other writing projects in mind and wasn't at all convinced that his should have priority. But I did promise to consider it.

The next day I ventured to discuss the idea with

friends whose counsel I held in high regard. One was a physician, another a nursing supervisor, both of whom had considerable experience of the problems attendant upon dying patients. They thought such a book out of the question. The American people were not yet ready, they said, for a treatise on the philosophy of dying well.

I know what my answer to Jim will be. I am a man too much concerned with the business of living, at least for the moment, to concern myself with the alternative. When I finish this book I have another in mind. But it, too, will be a celebration of life, not death.

However, I cannot help but think that my good friend is on to something. We are, indeed, a people who know too little of the natural end process of existence. We are a people who cling, at times, too desperately to sparks of life scarcely worth the keeping. The jogger runs tirelessly in an agony of exertion, hoping thereby to extend his sojourn on this planet by a few months. The smoker sacrifices the boundless pleasure and great solace of his tobacco, hoping thereby to add a year or two to his life span, forgetting that the year or two will most likely be added to a feeble dotage. And what of the thousands who linger on death beds with incurable diseases, wracked by pain and mad with senility, wanting to die but nailed to their faltering lives just as they are nailed to their beds of despair? Surely, there must be a better, more humane, more dignified way to reach the inevitable destiny that waits for all of us.

The libidinal arguments for living are, of course, of great intensity. Who, having read Ludwig Bemelman's "Now I Lay Me Down To Sleep," can readily forget the poignant lines spoken by The General who said, "I am well acquainted with death, Miss Graves . . . I die almost every three months and then I wake up and I am here again . . . Oh, how happy I am . . . a running child, a flag waving in the wind, a grapefruit . . . fills me with ecstasy ... I cannot imagine a paradise more complete and beautiful than this world."

But such effusions, stirring though they may be, are pointless when life becomes little more than torture or when the exhausted organism is ready for the final sleep. I recall a television program in 1974 known as the "Hellstrom Chronicle," an alternately provocative and patronizing documentary, in which there is a graphic scene in which the may flies are born to live but 18 hours. The commentator observes: "They accept the gift of life and gently say good-bye without all the torment man has in asking 'why?'" There may be a lesson in the may fly for all of us who spend too much time searching for life's meaning, unable to accept it for the gift it is, a gift that each of us must one day relinquish.

It is quite possible that Jim's book will yet be written and published, perhaps by him, perhaps by others. If it is, I shall read it with interest; I just don't see myself involved in the writing of it.

At Last,
Some Time For Loafing

EVEN AT OUR BUSY little Eden there comes a time to loaf and that time is August when the garden is heavy with flowers and produce and there's no longer much point in worrying about the weeds.

Loafing means sitting in a lawn chair under the twin cedars where you can watch yellow flowers which should be as tall as midgets, but are so topheavy with blossom they almost touch the lawn. Naturally, I could stake them, but that means a lot of effort for a warm afternoon. It's better to let them droop in their wanton but attractive disorder. The phlox in the same border stands straight and tall enough. The wild sweetpeas always find something on which to climb. And there's no pattern at all to the foxglove.

Loafing means tall, cool drinks (preferably with slices of lime) or perhaps a bottle or two of rich ale still glistening with refrigerator sweat. It means a game of cribbage and waiting until the evening cool for the horseshoe game. It means doing nothing more strenuous than looking at the big thermometer now and then to confirm your suspicion that it's in the 80s but not uncomfortably so.

Loafing at River Place means pawing through the

bookshelves for something to read that you most likely have read before, but years ago. It means finding lines in other men's books to fit your own mood.

Here's Thoreau, the supreme naturalist: "Many men go fishing all of their lives without knowing it is not the fish they are after." How apropos for River Place. A friend of ours says, "Any place without a river is only a stopover for me."

Or, similarly, Roderick L. Haig-Brown in "A River Never Sleeps" — "I still don't know why I fish or why other men fish, except that we like it and it makes us think and feel. But I do know that if it were not for the strong, quick life of rivers, for their sparkle in the sunshine, for the cold grayness of them under rain and the feel of them about my legs as I set my feet hard down on rocks or sand and gravel, I should fish less often. A river is never quite silent; it can never of its very nature be quite the same from one day to the next. It has its own life and beauty, and the creatures it nourishes are alive and beautiful also. Perhaps fishing, for me, is only an excuse to be near rivers. If so, I'm glad I thought of it."

* * *

THE MORNING HOURS have gold in their mouths, says a German proverb. In August it's more like platinum here where the woods nudge the river and the dew is so heavy that tears of it gather on the birches to flash like diamonds in the early sun.

A Certain Party once again is threatening to take up mulch gardening (I like the look of conventionally tilled soil myself) and is reading Ruth Stout's remarkable "How To Have A Green Thumb Without An Aching Back."

"Now and then," says Mrs. Stout, "there is a morning so beautiful it makes you feel that all the world, and heaven too, has had a conference and voted to create one perfect thing. When you have rejoiced in the splendor all around you, you close your eyes, the better to drink in the sounds. They are only birds, singing and calling from the trees — there is also music in the grass. You are afraid to take one step for fear you will tread upon some lovely and mysterious sound."

Mrs. Stout is given to exaggeration. (For example, she writes about heads of lettuce "as big as sombreros.") Yet I know what she means about perfect mornings. In August we have our share of them and they are almost all that one can bear. This morning ACP put the Rachmaninoff concerto on the tape player while I was drinking in all that outdoor glory. Take it off, I told her. The senses can accommodate only so much.

* * *

IN THREE YEARS we've lost chickens to coccidiosis, bumblefoot, a neighbor's dog and plain old age, but until two weeks ago we had never lost one to a wild predator. Amazingly, we've escaped raccoons, bobcats, foxes, skunks, civet cats, weasels, owls, eagles, hawks and crows, all of which like high protein chicken.

And now something is getting into the henhouses at night, snapping the necks of a chicken or a couple of quail and eating only the entrails. "That would be a weasel," says a friend who's expert in such matters. "They just take the blood and the viscera."

So I'm off in search of a trap. My friend tells me to get the "humane" type which catches the animal in a box of wire mesh so that it can be released, unharmed, elsewhere. At a large outdoor store I find an assortment of traps, but nothing that seems to fit a weasel. There's one trap there that looks like a steel version of a man-eating clam. I ask the salesman what on earth it's used for besides trapping elephants. Bears, he says. He tells me they sell a lot of bear traps. I don't wish to hear about it.

Finally, I'm forced to fall back on the mail order catalog. There's the very trap I want, a $7.99 number for taking squirrels, chipmunks and weasels painlessly. With it come instructions couched in rather graphic language.

"Avoid handling the trap and bait," say the instructions. "Use raw liver or chicken entrails for bait and handle them with wires or gloves smeared with blood." It all sounds primitive, but we've got to get that weasel. He's already killed four laying hens.

When and if we catch him — I understand weasels are notoriously clever at dodging traps — we shall most likely take him a few miles up river where no one keeps chickens and let him go. I hold no particular brief for weasels, but they must serve a purpose in the scheme of things.

Meanwhile, we're closing the henhouses up tight each night, blocking the ports to the runs. Maybe the weasels are doing us a favor, I learned long ago that the price of chicken feed is such that keeping a large flock is a losing proposition. Still, if I am to thin my flock I'd rather do the dirty work myself.

However, late summer's lazy days are no time for philosophy. It's a time to check the roasting ears and look for ripe tomatoes. It is a time to savor days that are like precious metals — the platinum mornings, the golden afternoons and the silvery nights when the burnished stars silhouette the firs, making them seem so much taller than they are by daylight that the river appears a frightened thing fleeing a canyon haunted by giants.

Making Ketchup

THE GARDEN'S TURNED OUT much better than expected this year. We have more than we can use of almost everything we planted.

I dry the black beans for soup. All one has to do is add onions and a bit of pork loin to them and boil up a soup far better than anything the Campbell people have ever concocted.

The tomatoes aren't much for freezing other than for cooking and I've never been partial to canned tomatoes. It seems the best thing to do is make ketchup. Mrs. Charlie has a lot of old-fashioned cookbooks with recipes for apple ketchup, cranberry catsup, chili ketchup, etc., but what I wanted was a recipe for plain tangy ketchup and I finally decided the way to get it was to take two or three of her fancier recipes and approach them empirically, playing around with the spices.

I started with seven pounds of ripe tomatoes which I cored and trimmed. I put them in a big pot with three cups of cider vinegar and added three big Walla Walla sweet onions to the pot, finally diced. After I'd cooked the mixture about a half hour I forced it through a sieve and put the remaining tomato and onion pulp on my compost heap.

The fine pulp and liquid went back on the burner and I added the following:

Two teaspoons of cinnamon.

One teaspoon of ground cloves.

One teaspoon of dried mustard first mixed with water.

Two teaspoons of black pepper.

Three teaspoons of salt.

One teaspoon of paprika.

A cup and a half of sugar.

It took three hours of simmering and a couple of teaspoons of arrowroot to thicken it. Then I sterilized some clear glass pop bottles, poured the ketchup into it and capped it with my root beer bottle capper. It's not as thick nor as red as Herr Heinz's product, but it's tastier. It was a lot of work for five small bottles, but it was worth it to hear A Certain Party proclaim it a good product. Next time I'll make a bigger batch.

Wanna Buy A Duck?

Mice In My Boots

IF BITTER WEATHER comes this year we're ready for it. The outside water taps are wrapped with burlap, the cabin's foundation is banked with earth and the chickenhouses are cosy with new straw.

Cedar shavings make good litter for a henhouse, but in the winter straw seems to work better and it is just as well. The man at the feed store says he can't get any kind of wood shavings these days. Straw at $1 a bail remains one of the few bargains.

I still worry about the wellhouse. Two years ago when we had a cold snap I put a 100-watt bulb in there to keep it from freezing. Worrywart that I am, I keep thinking when I'm not there that the bulb will burn out and Charlie won't think to check on it.

Even though the weather has remained relatively mild there's no question about it being January in the hollow. Early in the day the orchard is dressed in frost and the wind along the river cuts like a well-honed blade. It's a time of the year when I like to drive alone to River Place and spend a few hours doing the quiet things a man does best on his own.

Today I checked on compost heap and looked for rabbit damage in the orchard. I turn the tractor engine over to guard against vapor lock. I plant our "living" Christmas tree, a Colorado spruce. After considerable study I find a place for the pink dogwood my mother gave us as a Yule gift. There were also the fir seedlings which came with the holidays, gifts from the governor which may well prove the most lasting memorial of his administration.

Such piddling chores done, I take down my waders from the peg in the utility room. The right boot goes on easily, but as I pull on the left one my foot finds a soft blockage in the shank. I tip the boot upside down and bits of straw, tufts of insulation and a shower of dog biscuits come tumbling out. Nesting mice like nothing better than fishing boots for their winter quarters.

* * *

THE RIVER IS CHILL and too high, but I have it all to myself save for some mallards. There's not much hope of a catch, but it nourishes the spirit and I stay until my fingers grow numb with the cold.

The sky grows darker and while I fix coffee and a canned meat sandwich snow begins falling, chasing the fowls into their coops and setting the ducks to quacking as they waddle through the whitening grass. If the snow grows heavier and the temperature falls after sundown the river road will be treacherous and I have no chains for my truck. I know I must lock up the cabin and leave it to the mice and be on my way lest I be snowbound.

The temptation to linger is great. For years I have nursed the idea that to be truly snowbound in the woods would be a grand adventure. The pantry is filled with such things as corned beef and dried milk and I could always make my own bread. There is never a shortage of fuel for the woodstove and the library is stacked with unread books. Who knows what discoveries a man might make cut off from the outside world for three or four days?

Unfortunately, the duties and cares of the workaday world won't allow for such experiments. Someday there will be time for watching the snow pile up under the cedars and the icicles forming under the eaves. This is not that time and I make the long, lonely drive back to the city, leaving my place not only to the gentle mice but to whatever other quiet visitors January may bring.

The Long Way Home

WHEN THE END came there wasn't much choice. She was little more than an arthritic, cancerous bag of bones and she had to be put down.

It was an act of charity. The vet injected an overdose of anesthetic and it was all over in less than a minute.

We had Charlie dig a grave for her. We had wanted it under the new dogwood on the river side of the cabin, but Charlie didn't quite understand and he buried her under the maple at the corner of the garden.

And thus, after 18 years, her incredibly long life came to its merciful end. We burned her bedding and disposed of her plastic dish. She never had a collar or chain, at least not for long. Apart from a few snapshots, some home movie film and the footprints she left in the fresh concrete of a sidewalk back in '72, there will be little to remind us that she's there sleeping the longest sleep under the maple, not that we'll need physical reminders.

* * *

SNOWBIRD BOUGHT her as a pup in 1957. The cost was only $2 and the price, considering her bloodlines, was about right. She obviously was half springer spaniel, but nobody was ever sure what the rest of her lineage might be. Probably cocker, but that's just a guess.

Anyway, she was alert and had a rich, black coat with a snow white chest and a white blaze on her snout. Nobody ever praised her conformation, but then, no one ever ridiculed it either. She was what you'd call an ordinary dog.

We named her "Bunce" for an artist friend of ours and she grew into the kind of dog with which I can live best. She never jumped on you when you came home from work. She didn't bark or howl in the night. She was housebroken easily and came when she was called. She never chased cars and never bit anybody. The only people she growled at were the Watkins man and magazine salesmen who came to the door. All in all, my kind of dog.

And as she grew older she loved to hunt. She had the springer's nose and stamina and for 11 years I would take her with me in pheasant and quail season. She would run ahead of the guns in the draws and swails, charging into the thickest cover when she knew a bird was hiding there. She'd wait for the guns to finish and then retrieve the cripples. Best of all she liked to hunt after a snowfall, trailing pheasants through cornfield and wheat stubble until she would drop with exhaustion.

She never had a litter and she never learned to do more than a few tricks. Her whole existence was tied up with the hunting each fall and when I grew either too old or too wise to enjoy killing birds and gave up the hunting trips, a big thing went out of her life. I sometimes think I continued hunting long after I'd lost my taste for it just because that dog loved it so.

* * *

HER DEAFNESS began two or three years ago. Even then, she was an old dog.

All the dogs with which she had hunted died and she lived on. My father's Labrador outlived my father, but not Bunce. My brother's springer spaniel, a real one, died years ago. It got so that people who hadn't seen us for years would come to visit and would remark on the fact that we still had that old dog.

She kept remarkably well. Except for the growing deafness, there were few problems. Once, three or four years ago, she had a bad bout of arthritis and trouble rising. I doused her with liniment and gave her some warm milk with whisky and that was the end of it.

After we bought this place she enjoyed it immensely. She loved chasing the rabbits and squirrels.

When we poured the sidewalk she unconcernedly walked through the wet mortar. "Don't trowel the marks out," said Charlie. "It'll give you something to remember that old dog by when she's gone." I left the tracks and scrawled in the date.

The last summer she developed a bad bronchitis but the vet pulled her through that, too, even when we had despaired. But she did begin slowing down and we knew her days were numbered, hoped that she would die in her sleep.

She was totally deaf by then, but her nose was still good and her eyesight not bad. Winter came and her arthritis came back and would not respond to liniment. She developed a cough and skin cancers on her muzzle. Then the cancer spread to a leg and, for the first time in her life, she lost interest in food.

Originally, she had been Snowbird's dog and Snowbird made the ultimate decision. She took her to the vet and waited to claim the tired body. Then she helped Charlie bury her under the maple where the leaves pile up in a winter blanket, not far from where she once chased rabbits. The next Monday she would have been 18 and that, for a dog, is a long, long way to have come.

Thinking Of
Barrels Of Cider
Yet To Come

Solstice Insomnia

ORDINARILY, I sleep better than a log of hard maple, but the winter solstice finds me fighting a rearguard action with sleeplessness.

Maybe it's infectious. Grandson Jubal has an acute case, brought on by visions of sugarplums and the impending visit of an old gentleman in a red suit. We keep telling him the big event is still some days away, but there is a warp in the time sense of a youngster not easily straightened.

Hence, while Jubal tosses and turns, thinking on Christmas trees and his chances of getting that train, I lie awake watching the changing sky.

At 3 a.m. Orion swings by the patio window, his sword belt a brilliant cluster of gemstones in the dark sky above my neighbor's woods. I get out of bed, poke the glowing coals of the alder into life and jam another chunk into the woodstove. By the time I'm back in bed again only one point of Orion remains in view. A few minutes later my small tent of sky is empty save for a single star, the name of which I do not know.

When I was a boy in South Dakota I used to lie awake summer nights and think of the sky moving past with the precision of a vast parade. Now I'm older I realize that it's we on this verdant spaceship who are doing the moving, but the fascination remains the same. Sophistication does not necessarily breed cynicism. My innocent belief in Santa Claus, for example, remains intact after 50 years, undented by the scoffers.

Insomnia has its uses. Sometimes I use the sleepless hours to finish a good book. At others, I make entries in the cabin journal. Perhaps the worst feature of insomnia is that it plays hob with a diet. Toasting a muffin at 4 a.m. leads to a glass of apple juice from the jug I keep on the back steps for crisp refrigeration. And there's always the temptation to drink a glass of warm milk to induce the sleep that will not come.

* * *

DARKNESS not only comes early in December, it drops its canvas with surprising swiftness.

By 5 p.m. it's too late for outside chores and A Certain Party and I play a few games of cribbage, exchanging quarters and gloats over minor triumphs of pegging. Suddenly, there's a fearful racket from the henhouses where the chickens signal a problem.

I grab a flashlight and go to investigate, deciding against taking the shotgun, an instrument that stands beside the door primarily for use against moles (I am grateful that I have never yet had to make a decision about using it against nocturnal prowlers of the two-legged variety. In this country a barrel or two of buckshot is too often the solution to such problems, even when they are fired harmlessly into the air.) In the door of one of the coops I find my old friend, the great horned owl. He slowly takes wing in the arc of my flashlight and would be an easy target if I had brought my gun.

We have lost more chickens to owls than to weasels, foxes or any other predators over the years and I am pleased to learn that this time the flock is intact, although badly frightened. And inasmuch as the chickens are unharmed, I am rather glad I didn't have an opportunity to blast away at the owl. The creature must be terribly hungry to brave the lighted henhouses so early in the evening.

* * *

WE PLANTED the blue spruce nearly five years ago, a pretty thing of five or six feet. Today it stands a good 12 feet, not far from the concrete walk near the cabin where our old hunting dog left her pawprints in the wet concrete while I was pouring it.

We dress the spruce in electric lights and that is all the Christmas tree I need or want. But ACP keeps Christmas well and insists she must have a tree inside as well as the spruce outside.

The river people are all good keepers of Christmas. Our neighbor Charlie has been busy for more than a month, buying and wrapping gifts for a host of grandchildren, using his meager pension check for largesse he can ill afford.

It is a December of great frosts, but almost no rain and the river remains low, tempting few fish to enter it. I ply what water there is with rod and lure from time to time, but with scant hopes of a catch. I fish because I love the dark, cold water and because I know that until the rains come I shall have this river to myself, sharing it with only a few wild things that respect its brooding silence and my need for the serenity that comes to the fortunate man who is one with the woods, the quiet rush of the shrunken stream and the peace of the early dark that haunts the hills after the winter sun hunkers down behind them.

Charlie's Way With Words

HE'S A GODSEND to city folks like us these busy spring days. When we're away he keeps a sharp eye on the cabin and checks on the ducks and chickens out of what he calls the "inkabator."

Charlie has his own way with words. To him, a window is a "winder" and a potato is a "tater."

He's a man of great practical knowledge who can fix almost anything. He keeps his rototiller, chain saw and truck going with the worst assortment of tools I've ever seen, all of the tools forever rusting away in his leaky shed. "You can't keep things from rustin' in this country," he says, whenever you comment on his tools. He has no time for niceties such as cleaning and oiling saws and wrenches. He's always too busy splitting firewood, charging his old batteries or raking rocks out of his vegetable garden on the hill. Since Mrs. Charlie has been ill, he also spends a lot of time doing the cooking and housework and driving back and forth to the hospital.

Charlie not only looks after his burros, but fattens a pen of pigs, boards a horse and builds fences for people up the river. His yard is a menagerie of chickens, ducks, peafowl, goats, dogs and cats. His house, on weekends, is crammed with visiting relatives. He often operates on only three or four hours of sleep and his only worry in life seems to be that he might run out of snoose.

Like other men addicted to Copenhagen, Charlie will drive miles out of his way to get the cans with the freshest dates. He swears there's a difference between week-old and 10-day-old snuff he can detect instantly.

If there's anything Charlie likes better than a lipful of snuff, it's a belt of whisky. I don't think he ever buys a bottle. Mrs. Charlie wouldn't hold with that. But offer him a drink and his eyes light up before he steps outside to get rid of his snuff. If you pour him a stiff one, he nurses it for a time, belts it down and then waits for a second portion. If you forget to pour the second drink, he reminds you of your dereliction, saying, "I think I could use another shot of that."

Charlie, as you may have gathered, is somewhat of a character, but he's probably the best neighbor anyone in the woods could have. Nothing's too much trouble for him. He's strong as a bear and yet a gentle fellow who's great with children and compassionate with animals. Over the years I've wanted to do something special for him and several times I've suggested that he come to the big city with me for dinner in a good restaurant. Charlie doesn't seem to like the idea and I figure it's more than a countryman's natural distrust of the city. What, for instance, would he do with his snoose in one of those fancy eating places?

Defining Happiness

IN THE 17TH CENTURY the Chinese philosopher Chin Shengt'an was shut up in a temple for 10 rainy days and spent the time enumerating the 33 happy moments of his life.

"I get up early on a summer morning," wrote Chin, "and see people sawing a large bamboo pole under a mat shed, to be used as water pipe. Ah, is this not happiness?"

Or, "To cut with a sharp knife a bright green watermelon on a big scarlet plate of a summer afternoon. Ah, is this not happiness?"

Some of Chin's happy moments seemed of little consequence. For instance, opening a window to "let a wasp out of the room" wouldn't quite do it for me. Others, to my Western mind, seem downright frivolous. "To see one's kite line broken," is not my idea of ecstasy.

It disturbs me that Chin could come up with only 33 happy moments. And he had 10 days in which to reflect on them. In just one day here at River Place I can do better than that. But I do like Chin's way of putting them down. I tried it the other evening and it went like this:

To wake at night and see a single star winking impishly between the boughs of the twin cedars. Ah, is this not happiness?

Watching A Certain Party come from the garden with an armload of spring rhubarb as red and green as a box of Christmas decorations. Ah, is this not happiness?

To wake early in the morning and sit over coffee watching a tanager outside the window all but standing on his head to steal a sip of nectar from the humming-bird's feeder. Ah, is this not happiness?

Standing by the chicken coop with my friend, Charlie, we suddenly see two of the great bald eagles which live high in the fir trees on Snowbird's ridge come gliding lazily over us, their white heads glinting against the sky. Ah, is this not happiness?

Or, to wake at night and read for a while. Then, to walk outside in my bare feet on the wet grass and see the sky ablaze with the stars presaging a fair day on the morrow. Ah, is this not happiness?

There are easily a half-a-hundred such moments in almost any waking day in the woods near the river. I can't recall having tried to count them before.

Lying in bed early of an evening reading John Wain's biography of Samuel Johnson and thinking about that great, tormented genius of English letters. Ah, is this not, etc., etc.?

A group of friends come from the city to help me with the building of the latest addition to the cabin. We work hard for a few hours and then stop for a glass of ale and a sandwich. Ah, is that not happiness?

Very early we work in the garden, planting beans and corn in the rich, warm loam and feeling the goodness of it in our fingers. Ah, is that not happiness?

I try making my first angel food cake from scratch and it fails to rise. I grieve over the 14 eggs, but A Certain Party tells me we will make another one next week and she will help me determine where I went wrong. Ah, is this not happiness?

At dinnertime we feast on beef burgundy and an assortment of good cheeses, all washed down with a white bordeaux, followed in turn by snifters of brandy. Ah, is this not happiness?

Dog tired at night we must check on the baby chicks and the Spitzhofen hen before we can retire. We stumble out to the henhouse and all is well. Ah, is that not happiness?

If Chin Shengt'an were alive today I'd like to show him how easy it is to count the happy moments in our days. It was Goethe who defined happiness as a state half way between ecstasy and contentment, not a bad definition. As for the happy moments, I like to think of them as those fleeting bits of time when the spirit is wedded to the senses and life is a poem to be read over and over again.

Mrs. Charlie Leaves Us

IT'S BEEN a fitful August. What with the chill and the rain the garden makes a poor show. It's a fitting counterpoint to the sad news that Mrs. Charlie has finally given up the unequal struggle against heart disease and diabetes.

Charlie, a gregarious man always starved for company, is desolate. Their marriage was long and fruitful — four children, nine grandchildren, two great-grandchildren — and his wife's passing has left a crater in his life.

When we came to the river four years ago, Mrs. Charlie was already battling the rigors of heart disease. She went often to hospital, but between those spells managed a brave front. She gave generously of what energy she had to babysit her grandchildren. Her house was full of love and caring. She lavished affection on all living things. Besides her progeny, there were her flowers and her hummingbirds, horses, dogs, cats, chickens, pigs and even a pair of donkeys. Knowing that her days were numbered, she liked a lot of life around her.

She seemed to know she didn't have much time. On several occasions, taking her pills, injecting her insulin, crocheting an almost endless river of Afghans, she told Snowbird, "I'm going to keep alive until I become eligible for my insurance." She became eligible last April.

She was born in a now forgotten hamlet called Sunset, Wash., and early this summer she went 450 miles home to die. The undertaker said there never had been so many flowers at a funeral. She would have liked that. She was crazy about flowers. Her given name was Juanita May and she was only 62.

Finding The Killer

IT WAS MORE than a year ago that our baby chicks and ducklings began disappearing. We put it down at first to a fox Jon had seen by a brushpile across the road.

But when we found laying hens dead in the coops, their heads missing and their bodies eviscerated from the neck down, I talked to Tom McAllister about the problem.

"That's the way a weasel kills," said the naturalist. "You'll have to set a trap."

We tried traps. Not only box traps baited with fresh liver, but the ugly, steel-jawed traps we hate to use, but tried in desperation. Nothing. Weeks would go by and the predator would strike again. Whatever it was, it was jeering at my trapping efforts.

And then the other night Jon walked down by the chicken run with a flashlight and caught the nocturnal killer at work. He couldn't have been more surprised.

Next day, I talked with my consultant. I told him my favorite naturalist had let me down, given me some bum information. It hadn't been a weasel at my chickens after all.

"If it wasn't a weasel, it was a great horned owl,"

said McAllister. "They kill in the same way."

That's exactly what it was. A huge owl that invades the coop after midnight and before cockcrow to feast on my hens.

I asked McAllister if it would be legal to shoot or trap it. "Yes," he said, "if it's killing your chickens." But he went on to tell me how I could catch it alive by padding a steel trap and putting it atop a post. "An owl will sit and look over the lay of the land before it comes into the coop," he explained. "You can catch it and release it somewhere else."

So far, the owl hasn't been back. I hope it is finding mice in abundance and will leave us alone. I don't like the idea of trapping wild things, even if I can manage to do it without killing.

Summer's Aging Finery

STAGESTRUCK SUMMER is loathe to depart this year. She mopes around like an old dog who's found a spot he likes by the cookstove and isn't about to give it up.

Not that we mind. Her fading charms still suffuse us with warmth and stir living things from the sun-dappled earth. She's the queen of the seasons and if she wishes to linger a bit longer, autumn can wait while she preens and primps and parades her aging finery.

And yet, like a down-at-the-heels guest, she is making a real stay of it. October is hard upon us and the new chill in the night air suggests the leaves are tired, ready to shed their chlorophyll and show their fall colors. Already the maples reveal occasional patches of gold and the dogwood leaves blush pink. One gets the idea that what is left of summer is so fragile that one cold front could drive it away with the feeblest of storms.

Like many fragile things, however, it is made of lovely stuff. The gossamer of spiderwebs stretches between limbs of the willow, reminiscent of what the Germans call "Altweibersommer." The "old wives' summer" comes in those late, silver-sheened September days when the work of the spiders is said to be like the floss spun by old women into fine cloth. The air is as heady as fortified wine and the dew drips like spilled ale from the trees long after sunrise. "Look at that vine maple," I tell A Certain Party. "It's sweating like a Greek wrestler." She tells me it isn't a very pretty simile, which it isn't. It's just how the image strikes me in this precious slice of time sandwiched between two seasons.

*   *   *

THOSE WHO FIND portents of "hard winters" or "easy winters" in the evidence of nature might ponder the thick run of spawning salmon in the pools below our place this year.

It is a commonplace after mid-September to see the dying salmon milling about in the rapids and threshing out their nests in the gravel beds, the last act in a drama at once sad and thrilling. Never have I seen the Chinook run as heavy as it is this year. It must have been like this early in the century before the coming of the hydro-electric dams when the oldtimers say they were "stacked like cordwood" in the tributaries of the Columbia.

Bruised with ghostly white, they gasp out the macabre procedure that has as much to do with life as it does with death. They fight for territory until the very end, snapping at the tails of intruders. They line up in squads, platoons, even companies, treading water, always pointed upstream, waiting their turns to deposit eggs or milt and then die.

Other creatures wait for the carcasses. It's the only time of year we see the sea gulls at River Place. Like the bears and the crayfish and the scavengers, they wait their turn to get at the autumnal banquet.

It is the saddest spectacle in nature and has the same fascination as bullfights have for those of the Spanish ethos. But its pathos is ineffable. Nobody ever makes jokes about the exquisite torment of these dying fish.

LINGERING SUMMER does some good things in the garden, a happy place at harvest time.

I never thought the tomatoes would ripen this year, but it's happening. And while the corn I planted so early is nothing to brag about, the later rows are yielding ears for the dinner table. The late cucumbers are firm and flavorful and A Certain Party is still picking marvelous heads of lettuce.

Fall's flowers are nearly a match for those of summer. The yellow and orange marigolds are the proudest things in the garden. ACP's sunflowers, 12 or 13-footers, are a bit arthritic after the August rains, but their drooping heads are stern enough to stand guard over the marigolds. ACP picks a big bouquet of the marigolds for the patio picnic table. She won't have them inside because of their strong, musky scent.

The roses still bloom near the thicket where the young rabbits play in the evenings, but prolonged summer or not, there's a note of sterility around the place. Last evening the only winged things in the sky were the bats, working hard on the flying insects now that the swallows are no longer there to help. Watching them swoop and circle I thought about the naturalist who says modern man seldom looks more than 30 degrees above the horizon. Maybe that's why we so often miss seeing the majestic eagles, the skeins of wild geese and the grandeur of stars and planets.

Come to think of it, that's one of the things I like best about life at River Place. The business of looking skywards. It's not "modern man" who's stuck with his acute angle of 30 degrees. It's city man. In the woods by the river where there's always something on view, there's no danger neck muscles will ever atrophy. In nature, sky, earth and river are all of one piece. And happy is the man or woman who keeps a roving eye on as much of the feast as he or she can digest.

Winter, The Poor Companion

PALLID SHAFTS of February sunshine stream through the cabin windows and the gallon jug of wine glows with ruby incandescence.

The whole, as always, is greater than the sum of its parts. Poured into a glass the wine loses its ruby glow and takes on the sheen of a rosé. Still, unlike most roses, this wine has character. It was made by a shrinking violet of Italian extraction. Making wine comes as naturally to an Italian as does making love. Italian shrinking violets are as rare as Italian vintners are commonplace. Both, however, deserve our respect.

My Italian friend made this particular wine from 40 per cent Zinfandels and 60 per cent Granadas, putting them through a wringer before they go into his wine press, getting out all the juice of the grapes.

My jug of the wine is enormously successful. My guests are almost universal in singing its praises, save for old Roy who stops by for eggs and water, but he is a loganberry man. Chilling the wine slightly seems to enhance its flavor. It went well with the redeyed beef last night and it went down well today when we came in from the fishing, soaked through from an unexpected shower. Good as it is, I cannot help but think it might be better just to marvel at the way it catches and holds the sunlight in its depths than it is to quaff it.

* * *

OUTSIDE THE CABIN my own vines sleep the fitful sleep of the Northwest winter. It will be some years before they produce enough grapes for wine. Almost everything else is stirring and Snowbird, with the perennial optimism of the young, predicts an early spring. She cites the "red shriek" of rising sap in the alders and the clusters of daffodils pushing through the soil under the wild current bushes. There are always such harbingers to find if one cares to look for them, but I am learning not to hurry the seasons.

Yesterday the hens laid poorly, scarcely a dozen eggs. Today the nests are full of their beauty, including two giant double-yolkers. I put the double-yolkers aside for a friend who is drifting the upper river and knead a batch of bread. When my friend finishes his drift he stops by for a warming glass. I pour him a couple of stiff drinks and let him try the homemade wine. When he is ready to leave I wrap a loaf of my still-warm bread and give him the two outsize eggs for his breakfast. He gives me the smaller of his two fish, saying it is a "bad trade" because it is a lean winter fish not good for much of anything but the smoker. In truth, I am getting the better of any "trade." I have had the pleasure of his company.

* * *

MY NEIGHBOR CHARLIE isn't at his best this winter. Between splitting wood for his big stone fireplace and nursing his arthritis he has little time to help me with my building. Now he has an eye infection.

I go up to his house and squeeze an antibiotic ointment into his eyes. He sits in his darkened living room before his flickering television and worries a lot about his grandsons now that their grandmother is gone. He hasn't had a drop in more than a month. He won't even sample my jug of Italiano. When I think of Charlie and his malaise I get as impatient for spring as are the ducks. Winter makes a poor nurse and an even worse companion, even in this mild clime. And yet, without it, there would be no spring.

Giving ACP A Hand

THIS BIG, BEEFY guy name of Patrick has been watching Charlie's house since my neighbor fell over a TV set and ended up in hospital with two crushed vertebrae in his neck.

He seems a decent bloke and when he showed up and asked to fish the water behind our place I told him to go ahead. I did tell him I was curious about him carrying two rods as well as a net big enough to handle a marlin.

"You mean I can only use one pole?" he said. I told him that was the law and he said he'd always used at least two "poles" when he fished for bullheads back East. He knew nothing about fishing for steelhead and salmon, but he was willing to learn.

The incident was somehow typical of an April vacation peppered with cliches, both visual and oral. And the biggest cliche of all was the one I thought of this morning when the flicker started his 7 a.m. hammering on the bedroom wall: I'm going back to work to rest up from my vacation.

* * *

IT'S NOT THAT it's not beautiful by the river in April. A Certain Party's flower garden is a banquet of forget-me-nots. The silver birch is dressed in finery of

"At River Place We Mix All
Our Own Concrete . . . ."

newly-minted green and most of the orchard trees are in blossom. And less than an hour after the pesky flicker makes his morning wake-up call, the bluejays are scrapping along the eaves, making sure we're not still slugabed.

Two men come from the Public Utility District to switch our power from the old 125 amp panel to the new 200 amp panel. Little do they know it's taken me better than 18 months to wire the new addition and pass the electrical inspection, the latter an event that called for opening a bottle of champagne.

Anyway, one of the PUD linemen is perched on a ladder atop the cabin, rigging a johnny bolt to the new mast and looking across the woods to the river. "Nice place you got here," he tells ACP. "A nice setting." It makes us both feel as though all our work has maybe been worth while.

It has been a real working vacation. We poured the foundation for the most recent (and final, I trust) addition to our once tiny cabin well over two years ago. Now, seeing the light at the end of the tunnel (another April cliche), we're in almost a frenzy of labor.

Finishing the electrical work meant that at long last I could begin covering the walls and I've been nailing up sheetrock by the truckload. Someone once told me that a 4x8 panel of sheetrock weighs 67 pounds. After having wrestled a score of them into place by myself, I'm firmly convinced they weigh at least twice that much.

But were it just a matter of cutting and nailing sheetrock, this past week the job would have been done. In the spring ACP's thoughts turn to gardening and yard work and there have been one or two interruptions.

"Could you give me a hand stringing up the loganberries?" asks ACP. "Giving her a hand" means digging three postholes, finding three 6-foot posts, tamping them into the earth, stringing fence wire, raking up clippings and hoeing out 200 stinging nettle plants.

"I'm afraid we're going to have frost tonight," says ACP. That's a code phrase which leads to me helping her lift 35 hanging baskets of fuchsias back inside the cabin from their airy perches on the deck.

"It's time we had a doorstep under the east door," says ACP. After I've built the form and poured the step it's but a short leap into building forms for and pouring a 12x12-foot patio slab. And at River Place we mix all our own concrete.

And so it goes. Getting the TV man out to put in a new antenna means that he leaves me with 200 feet of coaxial cable to be buried. Moving the pool table from the shop to the new daylight basement means cleaning up the shop. One job always leads to one or two others.

However, it all goes well enough. The Auracana hen hatches her "chicks" which are really ducklings and won't behave the way chicks should behave, always wanting to swim in the water container and refusing to scratch for food. Charlie is making progress at the hospital after a rough time of it. And given a week back at work I should be truly rested and ready for laying a lot of linoleum while A Certain Party drops hints about getting the garden plowed for planting.

Doing The Lord's Work

THE LATEST ADDITION to the cabin is nearing completion and we hire a young man to tape and "mud" the sheetrock walls. For six days he comes each day to the river in his old Buick, driving 70 miles or more to the job.

He is a tireless worker and keeps pretty much to himself. When we offer him luncheon he is usually too busy to stop for it, but later munches on raisins or wheat germ he carries with him, alone. He carries a large Bible with him along with his trowels and other tools and when he leaves each night he gives us his blessing, but he does not inquire into our religious beliefs nor talk about his own.

After he makes his last trip to the river to sand the walls, filling the old cabin with dust despite a sheet of plastic we hang as a dust curtain, I give him his check and go to inspect his neatly done work which I will begin painting tomorrow.

I find pencilled inscriptions of simple scripture hidden behind the door casings and light fixtures. "God is love," is written on the wall in our new kitchen. "Jesus is Lord" has been left behind over the medicine cabinet in the bathroom.

In his quiet, simple way our sheetrock "mudder" is spreading his idea of The Word.

Our First Geese

IF SUMMERS, like wines, came in different vintages, one would be inclined to say this particular summer bids fair to becoming a classic not unlike the '47 vintages of Burgundy.

Indeed, the first tentative days to follow spring suggest, like the first sip of a young wine, the promise of fullness to come. Deer graze at the edge of our lawn for the first time in several years, unmindful of the dog. The cabin itself is invaded almost daily by other bold wild things. Errant hummingbirds, excited swallows, huge lemon-colored butterflies and a dozen other flying or crawling beasties make their ways inside and we have to release them.

However, two or three swallows inside the house don't make a summer and I must confess to seeing portents in more tangible things. The Chinese peapods are ripe with crunchiness, the corn is knee high well before the 4th of July and the river's pulse quickens with a heavy run of seagoing rainbow trout.

River Place has seen quail, assorted chickens, all sorts of ducks, wethered goats, sheep, burros and rabbits, but this morning The Snowbird came back from a trip to the feed store with the first goslings. If E.B. White likes geese, I figure they must have some good and rare qualities, although I am quick to admit I know almost nothing about them.

I have heard it said that geese are used for watchdogs (watchgeese?) in Europe where they set up a racket when an intruder approaches. I've also heard a lot about the force feeding of geese in Strasbourg to enlarge their livers for an abundance of pate de fois gras and I remember the years when Oregon's mint growers would keep them in their mint fields to glean the weeds.

That about sums up my knowledge of geese. Owning a brace of them will mean learning about them and learning new things never hurt anybody.

Casual Barter

NEIGHBOR ELWIN lost all his fuchsias in last winter's freeze, so A Certain Party offered him replacements this year from her greenhouse.

Elwin accepted readily, loaded his pickup with 15 or 20 varieties and headed up river. But the next day he was back — with a pickup full of firewood. The next day and the day after that he was back again, each time his truck piled high with butts of cedar and fir, ready for the splitting maul.

"Bread on the waters," said ACP. And that's generally the way it is at River Place where a crude form of barter is part of living.

The Norwegian couple who moved into Charlie's former house on the hill came down and asked for the loan of my concrete mixer. He's a giant of a man and he picked the heavy machine up easily and put it on his truck. When he returned the mixer three days later I found a dozen bottles of ale inside it. People seem to do things that way in the woods.

Sometimes it doesn't pay to ask questions about the lagniappes one receives from denizens of these parts.

A neighbor might drop off a package of fresh meat, for example. "It's from a road kill," he might say, and

you'll know it's venison. Just how the deer happened
to die along the road so far out of hunting season is
not a query one puts to a neighbor in country where
a bit of poaching is still a way of putting meat on the
table.

The same goes for gifts of salmon or steelhead. There's
no point in asking the donor from whence it came because chances are he'll fib about it anyway. If a man
has a good fishing hole he keeps its whereabouts to himself. And if he has netted or trapped an extra fish then
you, as a law-abiding citizen, would rather not know
about it.

This is country where the fellow who knows a bit about
plumbing helps the other guy fix his sink or install a
new water heater. The other guy, who may know a lot
about wiring, in turn helps his neighbor install a dryer
or yard light. In the years I've been on the river I can't
recall anyone every telephoning to town for an electri-
cian, a plumber or an appliance repairman. With the
help of a neighbor at best, we tend to do for ourselves.

It's been a fairly routine summer this year at River
Place. We remembered to observe Thoreau's birthday
in July, reflecting that he "took to the woods" for only
two years while we've stuck it out for nearly a decade,
admittedly with far more creature comforts than Henry
had at Walden Pond. Like Thoreau, we have learned
many lessons which only the woods can teach. But unlike
that rather stern, unyielding philosopher who made do
with only two chairs, we have never surrendered ourselves completely to the Spartan life, believing that there
are elements of worth in the cashmere of luxury as well
as in the hairshirt of denial.

Unfinished Project

COBBER WAITS for me each morning, leaping at the six-foot fence that surrounds his kennel, eager to be stroked, walked and fed, in that order.

The walk isn't long. Just down the river road to the heavily wooded area where my upstream neighbor finally built a small weekender. Cobber sniffs his way down the forest path through the cedar nurse logs where my neighbor's cabin sits high above the river. We always pause there to look at the water, check its height and color and spy on the herons at their early morning fishing. Then we make our way through the woods and across the plan bridge that spans No Name Creek and along my garden fence to the henhouses where I stop to throw the ducks a few handfuls of grain.

I invariably put the coffee on before I leave and by the time we're back it's ready. As I add the milk and a spoonful of honey we can hear A Certain Party stirring, aware that the dog and I have returned from our *Spaziergang* and that the brew is waiting.

We sit sipping our coffee, exchanging smalltalk about the latest mole damage or the weather while a noisy bluejay looks for food scraps on the deck and the last of summer's more persistent hummingbirds probe the fuchsias for nectar. After a few minutes, Cobber, too, gets his breakfast and another busy late summer day begins in earnest.

* * *

THERE ARE THREE projects I must finish before October brings its frost to the hollow. The first of these is the rebuilding of ACP's greenhouse.

It is the first greenhouse we have ever owned and, after a year, we have come to realize its deficiencies. For one thing, it was just too small, always near to bursting its breeches with greenery. I have knocked out the back wall, poured an extended footing and reframed the back section to add half again as much capacity. The newly framed area has yet to be covered with the heavy plastic. Meanwhile, I've put in floor drains, installed a 240-volt heater to replace the too-expensive 110-volt job and begun laying pipe for a fixed water supply to supplant the garden hose.

Once the greenhouse is done I've got to get the gutters and downspouts up on the old cabin. We've made do without them for some years now, but have had to endure flooding of the basement wine cellar when the rain or snowfall is heavy. I figure that if I can pipe all that water away from the cabin it will ease the problem.

And when that chore is done it will be high time to think of adding to the winter firewood supply. All summer long my good intentions of sawing and splitting a couple cords have played second fiddle to the gardening. The country dweller knows little of the urban luxury of idleness.

* * *

THE LONG WET SPELL that broke the drought, turning the brown grass of the orchard emerald green again, eased off on Labor Day, bringing renewed hopes that the languishing green tomatoes will yet ripen.

The hybrid corn is as sweet as cotton candy and the

cabbages are hydrocephalic. The Romano beans hang thick as spring grass and the beets and cucumbers are already pickled and on the basement shelves. It's the tomatoes that are the hold-outs. They've graced neither the table nor Mason jar. There are too few warm nights in the country along a glacial river.

However, at the moment there seems to be a freakish spell of warm air in the mountains. This morning when Cobber and I stopped to look at the river it ran almost white with snowwater. In the spring runoffs we have seen it change from smoky jade to the color of boarding house gravy almost overnight. And after flash rains, now that the loggers have clear cut so many of the streams in the headwaters, it often turns a chocolatey murk. A mountain stream has as many moods as a well-played violin. And yet this is the first time I have seen it run as white as milk, not unlike a river one might see in a bad dream or a primitive painting. We have to take a number of things on faith. Just as we know the tomatoes will yet ripen, we know the river will run clean and clear again.

The jacks are already in the stream and in a few days the silvers should begin their run. That'll be the time to suspend the building and odd jobs, shake out my waders and try my rod in the drifts above the falls where at least one fish lies waiting for whatever destiny our mutual fates may hold for just such a late summer encounter.

Playing A Big One

Gothic Times And Places

DRIVEN BY a westerly wind, the rain pounds at the cabin door with the persistence of a madman, interrupting our quiet game of Anagrams.

By morning the river is a churning torrent and the driftwood I had so carefully gathered and stacked 20 feet above the water is gone, swept towards the sea.

From dawn to dusk legions of hunters stalk the sodden woods in search of deer, adding a soupçon of violence to the already brooding woods.

At the river store they tell Gothic tales of gutshot deer, hunters who attack game wardens and frightened game run down on the road by log trucks. A Certain Party winces as volleys of gunfire break out in the alder thicket across the river, echoing along the rocky canyon. There is something in the hunting that brings out the beast in man and it is a time of strange noises, spectral sights and menace in shadowy places. The dogs bark late into the night and we sleep fitfully.

* * *

THE STAGE IS SET for an awesome All Hallows Eve, but when it comes it proves a delight rather than an ordeal.

We planted no pumpkins this year, but they would

not be denied, volunteering from the food scraps thrown in a chicken run no longer in use. Fed by the decaying manure, they grew huge from the strong vines and Jubal had his pick of half a dozen, none smaller than a giant's head.

Jubal selected one barely frosted with orange and too heavy for a three-year-old to carry. We put it on the kitchen table, scooped out the golden meat and then planned the sculpting of its visage with great care. Jubal decided it should be "mysterious, but not too scary." So his grandfather kept the snaggle teeth and slanting eyes, but curved the mouth into a grin more gleeful than wicked. Fitted out with a stub of candle he leers from the deck of Snowbird's cabin, more of a friendly, welcoming beacon than a goblin.

There is no parade of trick-or-treaters here in the woods. The homes are too far apart for the hustlers of candy and gum. We have some popcorn and fruit for Jubal who, not yet four, doesn't really understand the concept. For him, Halloween is little more than a jack-o'-lantern grinning in the dark.

* * *

HALLOWEEN brings us another treat. It is our one-time neighbor Charlie who drives all the way from the wheat country of Western Washington to visit again with river friends and join in the elk hunting.

Charlie looks great. Survivor of a dozen accidents, he has yet another horror story to tell. Fishing on the Clearwater in Idaho last month his boat capsized in the rapids. But he endures.

Most of the talk at this season turns to hunting. Fact becomes woven with banter. "I almost opened the elk season a day early," says one river dweller. "Just an inch lower and it would have been open." To hear another boast, you'd think his freezers were crammed full the year around with the fruits of his poaching. Poaching has been a way of life for these people for so long that even when they come to honor the game laws as they grow older they still like to talk a good poach. If truth be known, most of the older men seldom get a deer or elk at all, even in season, unless one of the younger men in the party shoots two.

It is a strange, almost forbidding time, this period that Keats called the "season of mists and mellow fruitfulness." There is rare beauty in hillside and charm in the decaying garden, but also an eeriness about the rushing river, mossy woods and quick gathering autumnal dark. These are nights to keep snug inside by the fire and let the pumpkins bear wind's force and slash of chilling rain.

"Delightful Accompaniments"

THE WINTER WRENS and chickadees breakfast in the dead ferns outside the kitchen window. The wrens are A Certain Party's favorites, scolding her with their insistent "chick-chick" as she goes for firewood. My biologist friend tells me their scientific name is "troglodytaes troglodytaes." It seems an ugly name for such a friendly bird, but it comes from their habit of nesting in dark, cavelike places.

I pull on my boots, make sure my fishing jacket contains spectacles, pliers, spare leader and enough matches to keep my cigar aglow in the January mists. From a basement rack I select a favorite rod. There's no need to call Cobber, the spaniel. When he sees me pulling on my boots he knows we are going through the woods to the river.

"The true angler's enjoyment consists not only in the taking of fish," wrote Thaddeus Norris in the "American Angler's Book" more than a century ago. "He draws much pleasure from the soothing influence and delightful accompaniments of the art."

Thaddeus found pleasure in almost everything that met his gaze as he trudged along streams with rod and creel: clumps of sugar maples, veteran hemlocks, laurel, moss-covered rocks, lengthening evening shadows, blue-bird, robin and even browsing cow.

And so it is for today's angler. The taking of the fish is corollary to the pleasure, not the whole of it. Indeed, there are those for whom the quest is the real pleasure, the capture anti-climactic. Such men know the silliness in Vince Lombardi's remark that "winning isn't every-thing: it's the only thing." The game itself is the thing just as fishing, not the taking of fish, is the thing. These are the men who come to know what Isaac Walton meant when he wrote, "I have made a recreation of recreation."

Like old Thaddeus, seemingly oblivious to the Civil War raging around him as he gathered the notes for his monumental work on fishing published in 1864, we shut out the world and drink in the wonder of the woods on a January day.

Instead of the whippoorwill which entranced Thaddeus, we have the amiable cavortings of the water ouzel. Fishing to us, even on a chill winter day when the wind nips at fingers and rain threatens with each passing cloud, is as it was to Thaddeus a "calmer of unquiet thoughts, impressing happy memories on the mind."

After an hour or so our thoughts are quiet enough. If there is a fish for the taking, it will be taken by someone else. The lure of warm cabin and warming brunch be-comes stronger than the tantalus of yet untried rift. And are not steaming coffee, warming stove and sustaining breakfast but some of the "delightful accompaniments" of the angler's art?

Year Of The Big Loaf

THIS SUMMER is going to be different. For the best part of 10 years we've tilled and tended, weeded and watered, fixed and fretted, built and battled and generally performed like plowhorses, reveling in all the sweat and extolling the dignity of labor.

No more. The building phase is done and it's time for the big loaf. As Aristotle put it, "The end of labor is to gain leisure." Here's a fellow who's about to cut himself a big slice of lazy pie.

Yes, I know about all the moss on the roof. I've already consulted an expert on mossy roofs about mixing pentachlormethane with linseed oil. But I may get it on and I may not. After all, the moss was there last year and the year before that.

And don't think I've forgotten all those holes our friend the pileated woodpecker drilled into the cabin wall this spring. I did nail boards over them to keep the rain out, didn't I? And one of these days I may get around to all the gluing and patching that'll have to be done. But not right now, not while the sun is smiling and the early summer fish are in the river.

* * *

WE'RE DEAD SERIOUS about cutting down on all

the work. So serious, in fact, we've been doing a lot of planning on the subject of taking it easy.

Of course, a few of our plans have gone slightly awry. Tired of cleaning the henhouses, for example, I sold off most of my laying hens, keeping a mere half dozen or "just enough to keep us in eggs." No nonsense this year about setting a broody hen with more chicks or starting up the incubator. But I failed to reckon with some neighbors down river who are moving to the seashore. The other morning they showed up with a New Hampshire hen and nine baby chicks. "They've been running wild in the woods, but we just couldn't move away and leave them" said the woman. I locked them in my spare pen. My flock of "just six" is now 16.

Things have gone better with the "lazy man's garden." I told A Certain Party that this year I was letting the Snowbird have most of the fenced space. "I'll just put in a few rows of corn and a couple of rows of potatoes," I said. In April I planted the spuds and corn. Of course, I did have to put in a row of Walla Walla onions. And I couldn't resist just one row of beets. (I liked them pickled in vinegar and sugar.) That was the end of it, except for a planting of Romano beans in an old chicken run and a few tomato plants. Naturally, when May rolled around I put in a second planting of corn. It wouldn't do to have it all ripening at once.

All things considered, however, I've been remarkably restrained. I do have to weed the asparagus ditch now and then and make sure ACP's strawberry patch doesn't get too dry. But four or five hours a week will take care of all the gardening chores.

* * *

THUS IT IS that I'm all set for a glorious summer of languorous days under the spreading cedars, sipping the longest and coolest of drinks, reading the best of books and stirring my stumps only to replenish ice or to shift from sun to shade.

True, I may, from time to time, find it in me to finish spackling and painting the laundry, to put a few more flagstones into the unfinished walk or bake a batch of bread. After all, I'm not a whittle and spit kind of loafer, but a lazer in moderation.

And I plan to do a lot of fishing without upsetting the lazybones program. One of those bits of decoupage on the cabin wall proclaims the saw, "There's probably no better way in the world to loaf without attracting criticism than to go fishing." But I won't be mealy-mouthed about it, the way a lot of fishermen are. Loafing is loafing, even with a rod in the hand.

It goes without saying that this reappraisal of labor vs. leisure will mean no end this summer to cutting and raking the lawn, putting up firewood for next winter, watering the orchard, grubbing out the tansy ragwort or mending fences. But I won't be breaking my back over such tasks or be going to bed bonesore, either. "I loafe and invite my soul," wrote Walt Whitman. I've sent out an invitation to the same part of my anatomy for the same kind of party.

The Swallow Box
Hypothesis

THERE COMES A TIME in March, just after the
bee balm breaks ground and the red-throated hummers
make their reappearance, that we begin watching for
the return of the swallows.

Jon has spotted some "scouts" already and it is time
to look to the nesting boxes.

The swallow boxes are a motley collection affixed to
cabin, machine shop, boat shed and other outbuildings,
roughly 15 in all. Old Roy built some of them when
he tenanted the property, and they are in sad shape now.
Jon built a fancy model with three apartments for the
shop, but the middle unit of the triplex has never been
used, swallows being egregious birds that shun immedi-
ate neighbors when they set up housekeeping.

Just as fixed as Parkinson's Law or the Peter Principle
is the Swallow Box Hypothesis, namely, that the returning migration of swallows each year will fill just as many
nests as are available, no matter how many or few you
may have. Indeed, most years after the boxes are taken
the swallows look for less desirable housing. For years
a pair has set up light housekeeping in an old aluminum
saucepan someone once nailed against the door of the
tractor shed.

Hence, I set out to build some new boxes. None of the handyman's guides are much help. Everyone seems to know that the opening for a wren house should be no bigger than a quarter. When it comes to swallows, you have to guesstimate the size of the opening. I figure it to be about one and three-eighths inches. After that, it's a piece of cake. Six pieces of marine plywood scraps and a dial saw to cut the port is about all one needs.

I put together a couple of new houses, repair some of the old ones and clean feathers, straw and fishline from the others. The swallows like to start afresh each year. I have a feeling I'm none too soon with this particular project. After the daffodils come the swallows are never far behind.

Last Will
And Testament

Williston Fish, a writer who lived to a ripe old age and garnered thereby a harvest of great wisdom, thought of wills as solemn matters.

And yet it was Fish who in 1898 wrote for Harper's Weekly a testament far from solemn that has been quoted perhaps more often than any of the more formal wills drawn by far more august personages.

You've all seen it. It's the will in which Fish leaves "to children exclusively, but only for the life of their childhood, all and every dandelions of the fields and the daisies thereof, with the right to play among them freely." He bequeathed to lovers the stars of the sky and the red, red roses by the wall and other such delights. And to those of us no longer young he left as a legacy "the knowledge of what a rare, rare world it is."

Such a testament, it seems to me, makes more sense than the finest of legal documents drawn by a battery of Philadelphia lawyers. Wills pose so many difficulties for many of us that we procrastinate about making them. Some years ago, when A Certain Party and I were about to embark on a long trip we actually went so far as to a visit a lawyer friend and talk to him about making a will. "You don't want a will," he said. "If you want your children to have the property at the river, why don't you sell it to them?" He was thinking about inheritance taxes and he meant well as a good friend. But it isn't that simple. A sense of order as well as a sense of duty dictates that as one reaches middle age it is best to get one's affairs in some semblance of organization. Life is an uncertain business and I suppose men make wills for the same reason they buy life insurance, a way of hedging one's bets while playing roulette with living in the chancy casino of existence.

* * *

In 1972, after I suffered a heart attack, I thought a lot about what life would be like for my wife and children if I were to leave them. For my birthday that year the Snowbird had given me an elegant notebook bound in green suede. Inevitably, I suppose, I found myself penning a holographic testament in its pages. Much of what I wrote is too personal for mention here, but the gist of my thoughts for A Certain Party and our children was as follows:

"Love one another. And try, although I know it's often difficult, to love your fellow man.

"Remember what Landor said about art and nature. Literature, music, painting, all the arts are important, but not so important to the good life, I would think, as is nature.

"Grab at life with both hands. Don't be afraid of it. Live it with gusto.

"And hang on to your dreams, no matter how difficult of attainment they may seem.

"I dreamed I would one day see Paris and the Parthenon and even the Taj Mahal. And I did.

"I dreamed I might one day build an idyll near a glacier-fed stream where my wife and my children and I might catch great shining fish newly come from the sea — and I did."

Then I mentioned a few regrets, a few accomplishments, the things that had seemed important to me all the way from boyhood on the prairie to middle-age in the forests of the Northwest. I ended my little "will" with a request I knew would be difficult to fulfill:

"Try to keep River Place for yourselves and for your children and for their children."

Would I change any of what I wrote if I re-wrote that testament today, a good few years later? Apart from specific mentions of my grandchildren — I didn't have any in 1972 — I think not.

Apart from our love, our all-too-meager store of accumulated wisdom and a few vagrant dreams, there is little any of us can leave to our heirs. Most of us have little in the way of stocks and bonds, vast property holdings, hefty bank accounts and chests of jewels with which to burden our children. That is certainly true in our case where the most valuable thing we own is our freehold on those few acres that border on a timeless stream.

It is a good thing that the one unencumbered bit of property we have to leave behind us is made up of intangibles as well as its physical features. And it is an even better thing that our children have the same almost sacred feeling about it as do we.

As a newspaperman I came to know the late Senator Wayne Morse of Oregon fairly well. In one of our chats over the years he told me of a fellow U.S. senator, a Republican from Minnesota, who was planting trees for his grandchildren. It struck me as a wonderful idea. What better legacy for anyone than a burgeoning woodlot, a flourishing tree farm, a dynamic forest, not only gaining material value with the years, but providing shelter for wildlife, windfall firewood for the gathering and an ever increasing dimension of beauty for all who look upon it?

Enamored though I was of the idea, I have never been

able to plant any extensive stand of trees for my grandchildren, but A Certain Party and I have done the next
best thing. Each year we add a tree or two to our orchard
and we carefully husband those we've nurtured in past
years. It is a standing joke among us that although the
trees bear small fruit at present our grandchildren will
harvest bountiful crops of apples, peaches, cherries and
plums. As I spray, prune and water my fruit trees I have
visions of Jubal one day operating a cider press to put
down barrels of apple juice and my granddaughter,
Shaniko, one day making cherry pies.

We rarely cut a tree of any kind at River Place and
A Certain Party has planted dozens of seedlings over
the decade or so we've been developing the screen of
trees along the river road designed to cut down road
noise and increase our sense of privacy. Similarly, on
the ridge across the road, trees are seldom felled. The
Snowbird thinks of each tree as a legacy for her son
and her acreage is so large that it could well be that
at least one of my grandchildren will one day own a
small forest.

Such then are our tenuous ideas about the future of
the place we have built in the woods. When my children
and grandchildren read this book I believe they will find
in it the one indelible message I set down nearly a decade
ago in a considered moment of solemnity — try to keep
River Place for yourselves and your children and their
children. The place they are able to keep may be quite
different from the one I have known, but I have an abid-
ing conviction that the dream, in some form or other,
will endure.

Getting It Up To Date

THE PIECES in this book are based on observations of rural living over the past 10 years and do not reckon with the immutable laws of change.

Some things remain fixed. Our conviction that people can come closer to lives of tranquility and fulfillment "away from it all" is steadfast.

The fact remains, however, that some of what we have treasured at River Place has vanished. Other things are threatened. There are moments of realization that we could lose it all, save the memories. Shortsighted timber interests have continued to pollute our river with their clearcutting practices in its upper reaches. Real estate developers have chiseled away at the remaining stretches of forest. Property taxes are rising beyond realistic appraisals. Population pressures have brought ever more people to share what isn't really ours, no matter how possessive we may feel about it. We cling to a hope that our grandchildren may yet inherit a legacy of woods and stream, knowing that hope may be fleeting.

Change has come for both the people and the other fauna discussed in this book. Our friend Charlie is beset with more and more problems in his declining years. Old Roy, at last report, was living in a "home" for those

Snowbird And Jubal Amid The Not-So-Alien Corn

in their dotage. The Snowbird, who came to the woods
for a time to live, has gone back to the city, but continues
to spend weekends with us. Jon keeps building and tends
his burgeoning grape vines. Jubal, now quite the young
man, helps The Snowbird with her endless gardening.

Our once proud flock of chickens has been reduced
to a more manageable coop of seven hens which provide
quite enough eggs. The ducks, at least for the nonce,
are gone. We lost our original pair of geese, but they've
been supplanted by Hans and Gretel, a brace of even
feistier geese which terrorize Cobber and make feinting
attacks on all our visitors.

The fish runs are obviously somewhat diminished from
what they were a decade ago, a condition common to
most Northwest streams. Our once sacrosanct canyon appears about to be invaded by a new tenant who has
apparently purchased a parcel of land on the long desert-
ed far bank of the river.

Happily, most of what is dear to us at River Place
endures, even flourishes. The tiny apple trees I set out
in '72 are now great spreading trees more than 20 feet
tall. The plum and cherry trees are bearing decent har-
vests of fruit. The asparagus ditch, dug up by the chickens for four or five years running, has finally been fenced
and is yielding a crop. Once again the vegetable garden
is in full production.

The swallows return each spring in seemingly increasing numbers. The sapsuckers continue to harry the birch
trees and an extremely pestiferous fellow known 'as a
pileated woodpecker continues boring holes in our cabin
now that he's reduced his favorite cedar tree to something resembling a Swiss cheese.

Best of all, the basic elements are unsullied. The water
from our deep well runs sweet and pure. The air is a
tonic. Despite the clearcutting in the headwaters, the
river retains its capacity for cleansing itself with its

merry, tumbling song. The sun still embraces the earth, the earth reaches out to the gentle rains, the deep woods with their tall first grasp for the sky and on rare days the bald eagles yet clutch at the blue heavens in a thrust for the adventure that is surely part of our continuing search for serenity.